# A CELTIC ODYSSEY

Anthony Gibson

ryelands

First published in Great Britain in 2009

ISBN 978 1 906551 14 8

**RYELANDS**
Halsgrove House,
Ryelands Industrial Estate,
Bagley Road, Wellington, Somerset TA21 9PZ
Tel: 01823 653777    Fax: 01823 216796
email: sales@halsgrove.com

Part of the Halsgrove group of companies
Information on all Halsgrove titles is available at: www.halsgrove.com

Printed and bound by Short Run Press, Exeter

# Contents

*The author with Carmen - ready for the off*

# Introduction

This is an account of a journey in a camper van down the Celtic coast of Europe in the summer of 2008, from the most north-westerly point on mainland Britain, Cape Wrath, to Asturias, on the coast of Northern Spain, taking in Ireland, Wales, Cornwall and Brittany along the way.  It was written as I went along, usually at intervals of about two days, and was posted as a blog on the internet.

I'd had the idea of this "Celtic Odyssey", as I called it, a couple of years previously, when thinking about what I might do both to celebrate my planned early retirement from the NFU, and make the most of it.  It sprang from a desire to reconnect with my Celtic roots, and from my love of the craggy mountains, desolate moors, beetling cliffs, sweeping beaches and pounding seas which characterise Europe's western seaboard. It had no serious academic dimension.

I do not intend to get involved in the debate over whether the Celts were a defined race, originating in central Europe and dominating the continent before first the Romans and then the Anglo Saxons pushed them to its outermost fringe, or whether they were a much broader assortment of iron age tribes, given a historical identity by medieval (and later) romantics. Suffice it to say that whoever the people were who dominated Europe before the Romans, they were undoubtedly gradually pushed westwards. To a large extent the evidence will speak for itself. If there are clear cultural similarities between, say, Gijon and Galway, then the case that these similarities stem from a shared cultural ancestry becomes that much stronger.

If I happened to spot themes that either connected or differentiated between the various Celtic races, then so be it.  But I was really much more interested in drinking in the views, playing the odd round of golf on some remote Celtic links, sampling the local beers, catching the occasional wave and generally getting a feel for the places I was visiting.

I bade my farewells to the NFU on a sunny Friday afternoon, and headed off to Stratford-upon-Avon for a round of golf with the Director General of the NFU and the Chief Executive of the NFU Mutual. I regret to say that I did not distinguish myself. It would be good to be able to attribute my incompetence to the mist of parting tears which was obscuring my view of the ball, but it would not be true. The fact was that my mind wasn't on it. I wanted to be home in Somerset, and wasn't sorry when the time came round to bid final fond farewells. It was at that point that I discovered I'd lost my car key somewhere out on the course. And, being a modern key, there was nothing whatever that the AA or anyone else could do about providing a replacement in any sort of reasonable timeframe. There was nothing for it but to ring my wife, Claire, and ask her to drive the 130 miles from Langport to Stratford, bringing with her the spare key. I will spare you the details, but it was not the happiest of conversations!

I whiled away the time wandering around Stratford, and got back to the golf club at about 9.15 – to be told that a kindly and observant soul had spotted the key on some distant tee and handed it in! What was it Blake said about "joy and woe are woven fine"? I'd got the key, but would have to break the news to Claire, who by now was just 10 miles down the road. All I will say is that, under the circumstances, she took it remarkably well. By Monday, we were on speaking terms again.

Anyway, it was not quite the parting journey that I had been anticipating after all of those years with the NFU. There were 36 of them in all, starting as a sort of junior speech-writer for the President, Henry Plumb, in the early 1970s, and moving on via the press office, regional PRO, county secretary in Somerset and regional director in the South-West to my final role, as Director of Communications. I enjoyed working for the NFU. Farmers are a decent bunch, by and large, who reward loyalty with loyalty, and there was plenty of flexibility – always provided you had the membership on your side – for deciding what to concentrate on and what else to do besides my core responsibilities. Thus I'd been able to write farming columns for newspapers like the Western Daily Press and the Western Morning News and produce farming programmes for BBC local radio, and reflect my enthusiasm for good local food by helping to create organisations like Taste of the West.

However, much my biggest claim to fame was the 2001 outbreak of foot and mouth disease, in which I appeared on local radio and television with monotonous regularity. To this day, I'm known around the West Country as "the face of foot and mouth disease" and I can tell, from the look on people's faces when they recognise me in supermarkets, that infernal visions of burning pyres and slaughtered livestock are being conjured up in their minds. Still, celebrity status – however brief and bizarrely earned – does have its consolations, which in my case included the OBE and an honorary doctorate from the University of Exeter.

Rightly or wrongly, the received wisdom among the NFU cognoscenti was that I was a whiz at public relations: "a real professional", they used to say. In point of fact, nothing could have been further from the truth. I have had no formal training in either PR or journalism. What I know, I have picked up along the way, using observation, commonsense and a certain amount of low native cunning. Nonetheless, in late 2005, when a vacancy appeared for a Director of Communications, at a time when morale in the organisation was at an all time low, I was the obvious choice. This wasn't by any means the first time my name had been linked with this role, but previously, it would have meant moving to London and the financial inducements had never seemed to make the game worth the candle. But by now, the NFU had moved its head office to the Royal Showground in Warwickshire, and the offer was a fair one.

I enjoyed the job, and hope I did it reasonably well. Certainly, even in the space of just two years, I think it would be fair to say that I had transformed the NFU's communications from one of its greatest weaknesses to a real strength. What I didn't like was the weekly commuting. Every Sunday night, I would lie awake, tossing and turning, sometimes completely incapable of sleep, and every Monday morning, I would arrive at Stoneleigh, grey and exhausted. By Tuesday, I would be fine, and I worked with some lovely people who made the job a real pleasure. But almost from the outset, I had resolved that I would retire as soon as I decently and affordably could, and that would be on my 59th birthday, May 9th 2009.

Once my pension lump sum had come through, I bought myself a second hand camper van – appropriately enough, a Chausson Odyssee 78 – which I christened Carmen, partly because its number plate starts with the letters BZT, and partly because the NFU's then Chief Economist, Carmen Suarez, is proud to call herself an Asturian Celt and had provided much encouragement to me in embarking on the adventure. Carmen – the van, that is, not the economist – had the great advantage of having a fixed bed, so that I wouldn't have to waste precious time each day on the cumbersome business of putting it up and taking it down.

So it was that on the bright and beezy morning of May 22, not without some trepidation, I climbed into Carmen's cab and set off to drive the 580 miles that separate Langport from Cape Wrath. The great adventure had begun.

*The way forward*

# A Celtic Odyssey

## SCOTLAND - MAY 25

I finally reached my kicking off point after two days and 680 miles. The journey did not have the most auspicious of beginnings. After bidding an emotional farewell to Claire, I set off at a steady pace, reflecting to myself that holding up the traffic would be a novel experience. Even so, the hand signals being employed by the various drivers who managed to overtake on the twisting road towards Bridgwater did seem to be particularly demonstrative. It wasn't until a builders' flat-bed drew alongside as we were crossing Westonzoyland airfield that I realised what the trouble was: my bicycle had broken loose from its moorings at the back of the van and was dangling at right angles, whilst the compartment below was swinging open, threatening to decant my golf clubs and sundry other precious possessions into the path of the following traffic. I swore and pulled in. I'd barely got out of the van to put things right before Claire turned up. For some reason I failed to understand, she seemed to find the whole thing highly amusing!

Thereafter, Carmen went like a bird – if rather more of a swan than a swallow. Unlike her namesake, she is built for comfort, not for speed! I stayed the night on a campsite near Moffat, dining at the Old Black Bull. No self-respecting hostelry in the Scottish lowlands is complete without (a) a reminder of some English-inspired historical outrage and (b) a connection with Robert Burns, and the Old Black Bull is no exception. A plaque on the wall informed me that it had been the HQ of Graham Claverhouse, who had been King James II's Commissioner appointed to suppress the rebellious covenanters in 1683. "Bloody Clavers", he was known as; and his exploits were "the Killing Time". The Scots are great ones for "nursing their wrath to keep it warm".

Which brings us to Burns, who, according to another plaque, wrote the following on a window pane whilst staying at the Old Black Bull: "Ask why God made the gem so small and why so large the granite?

Because God meant that mankind should set the higher value on it." As words go, they're not exactly immortal, and maybe I'm being particularly dense, but it's not clear to me whether it is the gem or the granite by which Burns thinks we should set the greater store. This being Scotland, presumably the latter.

Once I'd got past Glasgow, the traffic began to melt away, as did the radio reception. I lost Test Match Special between Perth and Inverness, so switched to Radio 2, to revel in the traffic reports. Sure enough, the M5 was clogged from Michaelwood services to Clevedon. How very glad I was not to be caught up in that lot. But as I was driving along a completely deserted A838 (which is actually a single track road with passing places) on the shores of Loch Shin, even Radio 2 disappeared. So I pressed the 'search' button, and was eventually rewarded with what I took to be a song in Gaelic. This turned out to be Isles FM and its "Drive time programme". Drive time, in the Western Isles?! "Boat Time" would be more like it.

Durness (pronounced as in 'furnace') turned out to be a joy: an oasis of understated civilisation in the midst of an elemental landscape. The campsite is directly above a handsome beach called Sango Sands, with the mountains behind, and sea lochs on either side. John Lennon used to come on holiday here as a child, a fact which is commemorated in the handsome, new (and no doubt massively EU funded) 'John Lennon Community Hall'.

I finally reached Cape Wrath (pronounced with a short 'a' as in 'rat') yesterday lunchtime, after a bike ride, a ferry crossing and a hair-raising 11 mile minibus ride along the narrow twisting road that was constructed for the building of the lighthouse in the early nineteenth century. I know that, thanks to the minibus driver, David Hirn, who knows everything there is to know about the most north westerly point on the British mainland and its lighthouse, and has even written a book on the subject called "A Light in the Wilderness".

And a wilderness is what it is. No-one lives on the Cape Wrath peninsular. It is a vast expanse of moorland, mountain and rock which has the dubious distinction of being the only military range in Europe where live 500 pound bombs can be dropped. Happily, these are aimed at a small island just offshore, rather than at the Cape itself, and not on a bank holiday week-end. The regular pounding has made little visual impact. This is a landscape more than capable of shrugging off anything that mere man can throw at it.

We were given an hour to wander around the lighthouse, admire the towering cliffs and watch the arctic terns fishing for their lunch. I had taken the precaution of bringing a picnic, which I ate (and drank!) in the shelter of the lighthouse walls. The sun was above and the steel-blue Atlantic below and here I was, in the most remote corner of mainland Britain. If my journey offers any better moments, they'll have to be pretty good.

*At Cape Wrath*

Later in the day, I played golf, at Durness GC, and this too was very heaven. It may not be the longest nine hole course in the world, or the most manicured, but there are some fascinatingly quirky holes, and one very good one – the par 5 6th which curves its way around Loch Lanish, just daring the over-ambitious to attempt a wood across the water, to get home in two. And the views are just stunning – of blue sea and the

*8th green at Durness GC with Balnakiel Bay beyond*

white sand dunes of Balnakiel Bay on one side and the mountains on the other. With crisp moorland turf underfoot, and the larks singing their little hearts out up above, it was a golfing experience I will never forget, and it cost just £15.

The only person I've met who has actually visited Durness is the Western Morning News' esteemed Farming Editor, Bingo Hall. When I'd told him where I was bound he said instantly "Ha! In that case you must go to the Seafood Platter. Marvellous fish, straight out of Loch Eriboll". And do you know what, he was absolutely right! I had a platter of lobster, crab, mussels and langoustines, all as fresh as fresh could be. It was a memorable meal to end a memorable day. By the time I'd cycled back to the comforts of Carmen, I was so mellow, not even the voting in the Eurovision song contest could disturb my equilibrium. In fact, I thought Terry Wogan made rather a fool of himself with his huffing and puffing over the Eastern bloc's policy of mutual support. Just because the Irish hate their neighbours, it doesn't mean that everyone else needs to!

But where, I hear you ask, is the Celtic in all this? Well, if truth be told, the far north of Scotland owes a great deal more to the Picts and the Vikings than it does to the Celts. Cape Wrath apparently takes its name from the Norse word hvarf, meaning 'turning point'. Which describes very well the precise geographical meaning of 'cape'. It is a headland that marks the dividing line between two seas; in this case the Atlantic and the North Sea. The only other cape in the UK is Cape Cornwall (which is where I learned all this), where the Atlantic meets the Irish Sea.

But going back to matters Celtic, I did note that the highest cliffs on mainland Britain, a couple of miles east of Cape Wrath, towering 900 feet above the churning Atlantic, are called Clo Mor, and that has distinct echoes of the cliffs of Moher in County Clare, which are the highest cliffs in Ireland. Someone will no doubt tell me that they are both Norse rather than Celtic in origin, but for the moment that is my Celtic connection and I'm sticking to it!

Apart from the obvious one, of course: the Gaelic language, which is still spoken by a few of the locals here. I thought I'd encountered one such when I clambered on board the little ferry across the Kyle of Durness, when the ferrymen said something completely unintelligible to a crofter from Fraserburgh, who is on holiday here with his wife. I met up with them again in the evening, at the fish restaurant, and asked about the conversation. He laughed. "That wasnae Gallic. That man was drunk. He hasnae been sober for the past five year!"

## POSTSCRIPT

I have done Durness a grave misservice. It isn't the 'John Lennon Memorial Hall'; it is, in fact, the 'John Lennon Memorial Garden', which is in the grounds of the hall and, if a little wind-blown, represents a genuinely moving tribute to the village's most famous adopted son. The claim is made – and I'm sure it is true – that it was his fondness for

*The John Lennon memorial garden at Durness*

Durness that inspired him to write "In my Life", which happens to be just about my favourite John Lennon song.

Anyway, when I get home, one of the first things I'll do is to download "In my Life", and for ever after it will remind me of beautiful, hospitable, elemental Durness – the village at the end of the world.


## MAY 27

Cuillins tower…

… above my campsite, which is routinely spectacular. It is at Glenbrittle, on the south west of the Isle of Skye. I am parked virtually on the beach,

*Campsite at Glenbrittle on Skye*

whilst all around are the aforementioned Cuillins. They look as mountains should look; impossibly high, impossibly steep, impossibly craggy and impossibly menacing: the sort of mountains your imagination would conjure up if you were reading The Lord of the Rings. These are the Black Cuillins (the Reds are about 10 miles to the north east), although they are actually battleship grey. When the evening light softens the jagged edges of the ridges and scree, it looks as though they've been upholstered in grey velvet.

*The Black Cuillins*

But if the mountains are magnificent, the mountaineers are much less so. Skye is overrun with people of all ages in lycra, fleece, leggings, fatigue trousers and, above all, boots. I haven't seen anyone wearing just plain shoes all day. For the genuine mountaineers, I have nothing but admiration. But the mountain climbers – the 'Munro Baggers' as they're known in Scotland for reasons I won't bore you with – are an unappealing lot.

In the pubs, they talk of nothing but their climbs; on the mountain they appear to talk of nothing at all. As I passed them on a brief foray up Sgurr Alasdair this afternoon, their faces seemed set in a mask of determination. The couples tend to walk in single file, about 50 yards apart – and that goes even for those who aren't married!

Anyway, I would rather they weren't here in quite such numbers. The campsite is jam-packed with them, the pubs over-run (or perhaps that should be over-tramped), and Skye – whilst undeniably beautiful – lacks the sense of solitude – of other-worldliness almost – of Durness and the far north western Highlands.

Last night I stayed at The Sands caravan park, at Big Sand, a few miles north of Gairloch. It is a big site, with every facility you can think of, set behind a ridge of dunes, beyond which is a huge sandy beach. As I sipped a glass of cool white wine and recovered from the 140 tortuous miles I'd covered to get there, I could see the mountains of the north of Skye blue in the distance.

But much the best of yesterday was visiting Sandwood Bay, the almost legendary beach which is claimed to be both Scotland's most beautiful and most remote. It took me about an hour and a half to make the four mile trek from car park to beach. The track got rougher as it went long, although the hardest part was the final slog through the dunes. It reminded me of dear old Fred Rumsey, a Somerset fast bowler of the old school, being set to run up and down the dunes at Burnham in his cricket boots, in order to get fit for an England call-up. I think he managed about three, before setting off with his 'fitness coach' to the nearest pub.

Sandwood was well worth the trouble getting there. To arrive was even better than the hopeful travel. It is a huge crescent of white sand, backed by dunes, and behind them, the dark waters of Sandwood loch. At the south end is a rock stack, whose Gaelic name means 'the shepherd'. Just off-shore is a large rock, called 'the sheep' (although it actually reminded me much more of the rock off Cape Cornwall, whose

*Arriving at Sandwood Bay*

15

name I forget, but which is known locally as "General de Gaulle in the bath"!) I couldn't linger long, as I needed to make it to Scourie before the pub shut at 2.30, but I picnicked happily in the dunes, basking in the sunshine and reflecting on how glad I was that I'd made the effort.

And so back to the present, which is a bit lonely. They didn't have a hook-up available (all those bloody mountain people!), so I've no television, there's no mobile signal, so no phone or internet, the radio can't even pick up Isles FM and I've just blown up the front of my gas grill, in which I was warming a pizza for my solitary supper. Claire will no doubt tell me that I'm stupid and shouldn't have closed the glass door, but it seemed the obvious thing to do to speed things up. Happily, it was safety glass, and no harm has been done – other than to my pride, of course.

*The Shepherd and the Sheep*

## MAY 29

Mainland magic.

This is much better. Bonnie Prince Charlie and Flora Macdonald are welcome to their Isle of Skye. The song that was running though my head this morning as I approached the ferry terminal at Armadale began: "Speed bonny boat like a bird on the wing, over the sea *from* Skye."

As an island, it looks fabulous from a distance. But up close and personal, its defining features (apart from the mountains of course –

when you can see them) are biting midges and smelly self-obsessed mountain climbers. It does have one saving grace, as far as I'm concerned: a pretty little nine hole golf course at Sconser on the shores of Loch na Cairidh. I spent most of yesterday there, playing golf in increasingly heavy rain, there being not much else to do on Skye except climb a mountain, and there wasn't much point in that because the top two thirds of every one was shrouded in cloud.

However, though I say it myself, I played pretty well and my happiness would have been as complete as could be expected under the circs, but for one rude awakening. Second time around, I sliced my drive to the long second into light rough. I took a four iron, to move it along. As the ball came out, it was accompanied by two clouds – one of spray, the other of midges. I am now smothered in Autan, but even with that, it would be a brave man who took his supper outside in this part of Scotland.

Radio reception returned as I reached the ferry terminal. This proved to be a distinctly mixed blessing. The first voice I heard when I tuned to Radio Five Live was David Handley's (of Farmers for Action fame) familiar, grating, insinuating whine. He reminds me of Uriah Heep in David Copperfield.

The description "fuel protestors" has come to define a new faction in British politics: embittered, right wing, militants-for-anything whose sole purpose in life is to get themselves on the telly, in any and every populist cause they can think of. The harm that Handley and his fellow travellers have done in mixing the farming community up in this motley, unprincipled, far-right leaning, egotistical ragbag is incalculable.

*The first green at Traigh GC*

After that, the sunshine which broke through as I reached my sylvan campsite at Camusdarach, midway between Mallaig and Arisaig, was balm to the soul. We (that's Carmen and I) are just inland from a beautiful white sand beach, looking across to that wonderful triplet of islands, Muck,

Eigg and Rum! The coast around the little golf course at Traigh, where I played this afternoon, reminds me very much of the Scillies, with its white sand, crystal clear waters and low, rocky islets.

Yes, there are midges, and I swallowed a good many of them as I was cycling back from the pub at Arisaig this evening. But they don't seem to bite as much as those on Skye, and I haven't seen a back-packer all day – just posses of middle aged German bikers riding enormous BMWs.

*The beach at Camusdarach, where I swam on May 31, with Eigg and Rum in the distance*

## MAY 31

To travel hopefully

One of the very first guide-books I consulted in planning this trip was the Good Beer Guide. That wasn't because I intended it to be a 3,000 mile pub crawl, but if there happened to be a pub serving a decent pint of beer in the general vicinity of where one was planning to stay, well, so much the better!

Poring over the maps and the GBG in the long and lonely winter evenings in my stable-conversion alongside the M40, I came across The

*The pub with no beer – the Old Forge at Inverie*

Old Forge, at Inverie – "the most remote pub in mainland Britain". Now there's a challenge, I thought. The only way of reaching it was by passenger ferry from Mallaig, and the best way of reaching Mallaig was by ferry from Skye. Thus was my route determined.

The final leg of my pilgrimage to this outpost of inn-keeping civilisation could not have started more propitiously. It was a simply glorious day, I managed to find a car parking space big enough to accommodate Carmen's considerable back-end, and Bruce Watt, the skipper of the Western Isles, could not have given a more convincing performance as "jovial Scottish boatman" if he was being paid by the Scottish tourist board.

We crossed Loch Nevis and arrived at Inverie, on the Knoydart peninsula, shortly before 11. It is, for sure, the only way of getting there, other than a demanding hike across 17 miles of some of the roughest country in Scotland, or anywhere else, for that matter. The Old Forge was open, thank goodness. But I decided that a walk along the shores of the loch would make the beer when it came taste all the sweeter.

So it wasn't until around 12.15 that I finally got to walk through the doors of a pub that I'd been thinking about for months and had travelled – all told – over 1,000 miles to get to. "A pint of your finest Scottish real ale", I requested of the barmaid, with a note, if not of triumph, then certainly of the keenest anticipation in my voice. "Sorry sir. It's off", she replied.

"Off? Off? How can it be off?", I cried in despair. The senior barman appeared, jaded from a singsong that had gone on until 3 am the night before. "Yes, sorry mate. I tried tapping a new barrel but it almost blew up on me. There's some more coming over on the afternoon boat, so we'll have it back on by this evening."

But that was no good. The boat back left at 3. So I ordered a glass of white wine and a main course plateful of local mussels, which are among my most favourite foods, especially on a hot day with a glass or two of sauvignon blanc. Ten minutes later, the cook appeared. "Don't shoot the messenger", she said, "but we're clean out of mussels". So I had bog standard haddock and chips, washed down with a bog standard South African chenin blanc, just as I could have done in any one of 500 pubs in Scotland. The view across the loch, the blazing sunshine, and the fact that I could at least tick off "the most remote pub in mainland Britain" in my GBG provided some consolation.

The boat trip back involved travelling further up Loch Nevis ("the lake of heaven"), to pick up passengers from Tarbet. A sharply-peaked mountain dominated the sky-line. I enquired of the affable Bruce as to its name. "That'll be Sgurr Na Ciche", he replied; adding in a conspiratorial under-tone, "it's Gallic, y'know, fur nipple." I looked again at the mountain, and could immediately see why. It will for ever have a special place in my heart!

Back at Camusdarach, it was such a glorious evening and such a

*No prizes for guessing the name of this mountain!*

beautiful beach that I decided that an early evening swim would be in order. The water was sharply cold, but no more so than it would be at this time of year in the Scillies, and I splashed about happily enough for all of five minutes. When the sea is really cold, it takes your breath away. This wasn't in that league by any means. Still, swimming in the sea, in Scotland, in May. It's not a bad claim to fame.

Today, I have driven down to North Ledaig, just north of Oban, stopping at Glencoe en route. The sunshine has been unbroken, and the mountains, glens and lochs through which I have travelled can never have looked more magnificent. I am, if anything, scenery-drunk, as mountain has followed mountain, loch succeeded loch, and vista unfolded upon vista. The road from Mallaig to Fort William follows the line of the West Highland Railway, which is presently featuring a steam locomotive, The Lord of the Isles.

Now that would be travelling in style.

## JUNE 2

Deafened by larks.

There are hundreds and hundreds of them here at Macrihanish, all singing as if their lives depended on it, and never so loudly, so it seemed to me, as when I'd just missed a putt on the sublime golf links which is

*The fifth green at Machrihanish – the Punch Bowl, with the Paps of Jura in the distance*

their home. This set me thinking. I play golf in the West Country at two not dissimilar links courses, at Saunton in North Devon and at Burnham and Berrow on the coast of Bridgwater Bay. Saunton still has a handful of larks; Burnham none at all.

So why the difference? I will offer you two possible explanations: magpies and badgers. I haven't seen a single, squawking, ill-omened, black and white nest robber since I've been in Scotland. As for badgers, which are equally responsible for destroying the ground-nesting bird population, a Google search for "badgers in Kintyre" drew a blank. If I were running Natural England, the first thing I would do is put a bounty of £10 on badgers, grey squirrels, magpies and American signal crayfish. It would give the disaffected youf something to shoot instead of each other, and it would do more for the balance of nature than all of their current policies (sorry, "strategies"), put together.

I am at the bottom end of the Kintyre peninsula, barely 15 miles from Northern Ireland. The weather is glorious and so is the view. I am looking out from Carmen's inner recesses across a herd of cows, to the golf course, beyond which is the beach and the sea, across which I can just make out the Paps of Jura. All it needs is a pub, and it would be the perfect visual metaphor for the life and tastes of A. Gibson.

These are by no means the only dairy cows in the vicinity. In fact, there are probably even more cows in these parts than there are larks. There are thousands of them, mostly Friesian, but still some Ayrshires as well, all producing milk for the local cheese creamery at Campbeltown, which specialises in something called "Kintyre Cheddar". Only in Britain would this be allowed. Cheddar is 500 miles away, for Heaven's sake!

But however ersatz the Cheddar may be, there is evidently nothing wrong with the profits. As I drove down towards the Mull itself this morning, the silage-making teams were out in force, and all with spanking new tractors and the very latest in mowing and foraging equipment. Dairy farming is evidently a glorious exception to the otherwise rundown state of the local economy.

St. Columba would not approve. The Celtic specialists will already have spotted that my 'Odyssey' has missed out what is probably the most important Celtic site in Scotland: the island of Iona, where Columba effectively established Celtic Christianity. I apologise for that. Put it down to my ignorance. I will return to Iona. In the meantime, I shall be making amends, first by being in St. Columba's hometown –

Colmcille (which is the Gaelic form of Columba), in Donegal, for his Saint's Day in a week's time; and secondly by following in his footprints, which have been carved into a rock not ten miles from where I'm sitting.

You will hear more of St. Columba in due course. Suffice it to say that in about 550 AD, a mixture of guilt and evangelism drove him to exile himself to Scotland where he eventually (in 563) arrived at Iona, to found the monastery that was to become such a force for Christian good. But the place where he came ashore in Scotland was at the bottom end of the Kintyre peninsula, just west of the village of Southend, and it is there that his footprints, his well and his chapel have been preserved. I saw them all, in this morning's glorious sunshine.

So why wouldn't he have approved of the cows? Because he expelled them from Iona, on the grounds that "where there's a cow, there's a woman, and where there's a woman, there's mischief". Not exactly PC, was our St. Columba. He and I have at least that much in common!

PS – Macrihanish is the most wonderful golf course. I had been looking

*The rather daunting view from the first tee at Machrihanish – the line is directly across the beach and I am happy to report that my drive safely found the fairway*

forward to playing it for 30 years, and it didn't let me down. The greens in particular are magnificent. They are huge and rolling, like an Atlantic swell. If only my brother Chippy had still been alive to play it with me, my happiness would have been complete. In fact, we would probably have completed three circuits. But I felt that he was there with me in spirit.

## JUNE 4

Haste me back.

It is my last night in Scotland, and I shall be sorry to leave. Apart from one wet day on Skye, the sun has shone throughout and I have received nothing but kindness from all the people I have met.

And never more so than this morning, when I turned up unannounced at Britain's only 12 hole golf course, at Shiskine on Arran, to enquire whether there was any possibility of a game. Seeing that I was on my own, James and his wife Greta invited me to play with them, and as they have been members there for 41 years, there was plenty of local knowledge for me to draw upon! The course was laid out in 1896 and is deeply old-fashioned, with lots of blind holes, but the fairways were burnished, the greens keen and the views breathtaking.

*One of the most famous views in golf – the 4th green at Shiskine*

Arran is an island of two halves – wild and mountainous to the North, gentler and more fertile to the South. It is a beautiful place, with an appeal all of its own. I camped at Lochranza in the north, having come across from Kintyre on the little ferry. I can't say I detected many Celtic echoes – for much of its history the island was controlled by the Norwegians – but I'm glad I visited.

There was a nasty moment this morning, when the otherwise impeccably reliable Carmen refused to start. I turned the key and nothing happened. Not once, but several times. Eventually, and for no apparent reason, she changed her mind and decided to go. I set off with a sigh of relief, although a seed of doubt had been sown, and I suppose it was inevitable that I should find myself first onto the ferry to the mainland, parked right up against the bow door, so that if Carmen failed to start when we got to the other side, no-one could leave the ship! My heart was in my mouth as I turned the key, and I was the most relieved man in Ardrossan when she burst into life.

This evening, I'm staying at a 'holiday park' at Prestwick. This has the undoubted attraction of being on the edge of Prestwick golf links, where the first Open Championship was played in 1860; and the distinct handicap of being directly under the flight-path of airliners using Prestwick airport. But it's handy for the ferryport at Troon, where I shall be catching the hydrofoil to Larne in Northern Ireland tomorrow morning.

Did I play golf at the historic Prestwick links? No I did not. The green fee for 18 holes is £115! That's the same as the annual subscription at Durness. Assuming I went round in about 90, it would work out at £1.27 a shot!

Beer is expensive here as well. A pint of gassy McKewans set me back £2.95 when I cycled into town this evening. At the Lochranza Hotel last night, a pint of Deuchars IPA (which was good) left me £3.20 the poorer. What with prices like those and the smoking ban, it's hardly surprising that many of the pubs I've visited seemed to be struggling. You wouldn't come to Scotland for the pubs. They tend to be functional rather than characterful. With Celts, the drinking and the company matter far more than the surroundings. Which is something I shall have to bear in mind in Ireland, where a decent pint is even harder to find than in Scotland, especially if, like me, you're not mad keen on Guinness or Murphy's.

So farewell Scotland. You have been good to me. When the sun is shining as it has been these last two weeks, there can be nowhere more beautiful on the whole of God's earth. Ireland has a lot to live up to.

*The ruined castle at Lochranza on Arran*

## IRELAND - JUNE 5

Irish impressions

So here we are in Norniron. Those of you who care for my well-being will be relieved to learn, however, that I do not intend to try out my "Rovverund Eeyane Peeaysleh" accent on the locals.

I crossed from Troon on the fast but dull (because you can't go out on deck) P and O hydrofoil, on a grey and gloomy day. The rain pursued me westwards as I drove along the coast road from Larne. I stopped at Ballycastle to buy some 'dulse', the seaweed that is the local speciality. It is purple, rather than green, and I sautéed a bagful in butter to accompany my sausages and beans for supper. If that sounds like a bizarre combination, it actually worked out quite well. The dulse was very salty, very chewy and tasted very much of the sea. Apparently, you can eat it raw, as a snack to accompany a drink. I don't think the manufacturers of pork scratchings have too much to worry about.

I had to stop at the Giant's Causeway. It's in the same category as Lundy, or Cape Wrath, for that matter: the sort of place that everyone ought to visit once in their lives, but to which, I suspect, very few ever

*The Giant's Causeway from above...*

return. The pentagonal and hexagonal basalt columns are indeed a geological marvel, but it's still surprising that it attracts quite so many people – over half a million a year – and from all over the world. There were as many Americans and Australians there as English and Irish. I wonder if it lived up to their expectations, or whether quite a few of them went away muttering, as William Thackeray did in 1842, "I've

*... and at ground level*

travelled 150 miles to see *that*". I put it down to the blarney. Whoever hit upon the idea of calling it "The Giant's Causeway" was a true marketing genius.

I wasn't disappointed, because I wasn't expecting to be knocked out by what my daughter Becky would doubtless have described in her younger days as "a load of boring old rocks". Anyway, I've been there, and that's what counts.

My campsite is just outside Portrush. The proprietor is a talkative chap. I asked him what was the best route to cycle to Coleraine, all of six miles distant. Ten minutes later he was still expatiating on the apparently limitless number of alternatives and I was still scratching my head. He didn't quite say: "Sorr, if I was travelling there, I wouldn't be starting from here", but I'm sure he would have done if I hadn't made my excuses and gone off to consult a map. In the event, and bearing in mind that it was tipping down with rain, I took the van.

## JUNE 8
The taste of Ireland.

Carmen and I have reached Clonmany, on the north coast of Donegal, just a few miles south of Malin Head, the most northerly point in Ireland. The mountains are to my left; the sand dunes and the beach to my right. It has been a sunny day. I spent this morning exploring the area on my bicycle, and most of the afternoon on the beach, even going in for a brief swim in the clear but chilly waters. However, my enjoyment was more than somewhat impaired by a plague of flying beetles, at which I lashed out in all directions, mostly in vain – an experience with which I am not entirely unfamiliar!

There is a lot of building work going on in this part of Donegal, much of it connected with the replacement of traditional, long, low, thatched

*A question of taste...*

farm houses with modern bungalows, built alongside. It grieves me to have to write this, but when it comes to vernacular buildings, the Irish have no taste at all. The old farmhouses may have been primitive, but they were constructed entirely from local materials and they are 'of the place' every bit as much as a granite farmhouse would be in Cornwall, or cob and thatch in Devon. Their replacements, by contrast, owe absolutely nothing to the area. You could plonk them down in any badly-designed new housing development, anywhere in the British Isles, and they would look less out of place than they do here.

The worst of it is that they are all equipped, not only with UPVC double-glazing, but with my pet hate of all pet hates, UPVC front doors! And all, to my untutored eye, identical. The unworthy thought occurred to me that perhaps someone from Donegal County Council had done a deal on the side with a double-glazing company. But it is extraordinary that in the midst of so much magnificent natural beauty, the modern Irish should build such cheap and nasty rubbish. If I was being charitable, I would put it down to the fact that the Celts are more interested in spirit and soul than in the arrangement of bricks and mortar.

There was a travel feature in today's Irish Independent on Cornwall. The writer waxed enthusiastic on how the county had benefited from "good planning". That will give you some idea of just how bad it is over here!

Yesterday, en route from Portrush, I visited a selection of early Christian Celtic sites, mostly around the town of Corndonagh. In unremarkable fields, up narrow lanes, one would suddenly come across a ten foot high cross, carved from a single rock, dating back to the 6th or 7th century. The crosses I saw yesterday all had narrow cross-pieces, suggesting to me that they were only half a step removed from the menhirs that featured so prominently in pre-Christian Celtic religion. But consider this: here you have evidence, not just of 1500 years of Christianity, but of a religious tradition stretching back into the mists of time.

Oh yes, and I also found a link with Scotland. The stone circle that I visited at Bocan was supposedly aligned quite deliberately to fit the east-west axis that joins the highest mountain in these parts, Slieve Snagth, with our old friends, the Paps of Jura in the Hebrides.

The pub culture may be being killed off in England by a combination of the supermarkets and a myopic Chancellor, but it is alive and well here in Ireland. Clonmany is only a village, with a population probably of less than a thousand, yet it has eight pubs, all apparently thriving. And that's not counting the "Rusty Nail", down here by the beach, where I dined tonight, most satisfactorily, on lamb chops and Guinness.

All the talk in the pubs is of the Referendum on the Lisbon Treaty. No country in the EU has done better out of its membership than Ireland. Very few countries' politicians and diplomats are regarded as being "better Europeans" than the Irish. Yet the latest opinion poll suggests a No vote, albeit by a narrow margin. In this respect, I can see distinct parallels with Cornwall. There too, they are only too happy to take Europe's money, and there too they would be only too ready to vote No in a Referendum, given half a chance. Put it down to Celtic contrariness.

Having said all of that, the Irish are lovely people: cheerful, gregarious and never too busy to stop for a chat, even with a complete stranger on a bicycle. Whatever the weather, and despite the hideous new farmhouses, it's hard to keep a smile off one's face for very long.

## JUNE 9

Cast a warm eye.

I am at Rosses Point. To the north is Ben Bulben; to the south, Medb's Cairn, to the east, Sligo. This is Yeats country.

This is a gentler part of Ireland than the wild and woolly west of Donegal. Yesterday, I set out to drive the 100 miles or so from Clonmany to Glencolmcille, pausing on route by way of what appeared on the map

*Ben Bulben from Rosses Point*

to be a minor detour, at St. Columba's birthplace, on the shores of Lough Garten. I set off at 9.30 and expected to reach my destination – the Tramore Beach campsite, near Glencolmcille – by lunchtime.

I made steady progress, despite the detour taking at least twice as long as I'd imagined. The roads became progressively more difficult, the further west I penetrated, but the thought of being at St. Columba's village, on his Saint's Day of June 9, having visited his birthplace, kept me and Carmen going cheerfully enough.

And, sure enough, I eventually made it to Glencolmcille (pronounced glencomkill) shortly before two. There was no sign of a campsite. I asked a local. "Tramore beach, is it", he replied. "There's no Tramore beach around here". I showed him the telephone number. "Ah, that's an Ardara number". And where exactly is Ardara, I enquired. "You see that mountain? It's the other side of that."

As the crow flies, it was only 15 miles or so distant. But what a 15 miles! The roads in western Donegal are diabolical. The entire landscape is covered in a blanket of peat, which subsides unevenly. This gives the roads the texture of a pebble ridge, coated in tarmac. At anything over 30 mph, poor old Carmen was in danger of trampolining herself into the nearest bog. The worst of it was the final descent to Ardara (which is actually a charming little town). For those of you who know the Somerset Levels, it was like the road across Shapwick Heath, set at an angle of 45 degrees and twisted like a corkscrew!

But our persistence was rewarded when we finally arrived at the campsite, more than an hour after leaving Glencolmcille. The sun had come out with a vengeance, and spread out before me was the most magnificent bay, backed by enormous sandhills, framed by grey-blue mountains, the sun glittering on the waves as they rushed in across the soft white sands. It could not have been more perfect.

*Tramore Beach in all its glory*

So it had all been worth it in the end. I had visited St. Columba's birth-place, which is marked by the most gigantic Celtic cross, and I'd laid myself down on his "Flagstone of Loneliness", where he used to recover from the exhaustion of prayer. It is supposed to drive away sorrows, and in the time of the Irish diaspora, the émigrés used to come here before they left, in the hope that it would cure them of homesickness. I'm not sure it has entirely worked on me.

Anyway, I reckon I've done my bit for the father of Celtic Christianity. I've been to his birthplace, his village, his abbey; I've been very near to the last place he set foot on in Ireland (near Malin Head); I've trodden in the footsteps that he left when he arrived in Scotland; and I woke up at the nearest campsite to the village which bears his name, on this, his Saint's Day. Perhaps next time, I'll make it to Iona.

Today has been warm but with a gusty wind. I stopped on the way down at Ballyshannon, in the hope of sampling that rarest of rare birds, a 'real' Irish ale (as opposed to the horrid mass-produced keg Guinness and Smithwicks). I managed to find the right pub – which rejoices in the name of Dicey Reilly's – and they did actually have Arainn Mhor, as it's called, in stock. "Course, it's not actually brewed on Aran yet", confided the barman. "They're still testing the market. This was brewed in Belgium". That's Irish authenticity for you!

Shortly, I shall cycle into Sligo. And tomorrow morning, I will wake up and be able to say, quite truthfully, for the first and probably the only time in my life: "I will arise and go now, and go to Innisfree". Now that really is living the dream.

## JUNE 11
A view to Achill – if only!

Only the bottom quarter of the Isle of Achill's beetling cliffs and rugged mountains is visible as I write. The weather is what the Irish call "soft". In other words, it's tipping down. Not that I should complain. This is only the third wet day in nearly three weeks.

Assuming the weather does eventually relent, I shall renew my acquaintance (I played there yesterday) with one of the most natural golf courses I have ever played. Achill Golf Club is laid out on linksland, behind a pebble ridge, surrounded on three sides by cliffs and mountains, and on the fourth by the Atlantic. The lie of the land is flat, but knobbly, – a bit like a supermodel on her back – providing all sorts of unexpected kicks and interesting lies – ditto, one presumes.

The scraggy sheep that roam the course appear to do most of the green-keeping. There is no watering and the equipment is distinctly Heath Robinson. I was fascinated by one tractor-drawn contraption which consisted of a heavy net, weighed down with four large tyres, which was being dragged across the fairways. It's purpose appeared to be to break up and spread the sheep-shit: not so much a tine-harrow as a turd harrow!

But for all that, this is proper golf. The course measures 3,000 yards for the nine holes and the greens – un-watered though they may be – are some of the biggest I've every encountered; on a similar scale to Machrihanish. I paced the largest of them out at 44 yards by 22 – almost 1,000 square yards. It goes without saying that I three-putted it.

*In full swing at Achill GC – it was not too bad a shot*

Yesterday morning, I got as close as I could to Yeats' Lake Isle of Innisfree; a vantage point on the banks of Lough Gill, about 200 yards away. I tried hard to be impressed by its romantic beauty, but in all honesty it is a remarkably small and insignificant island to have inspired such memorable poetry. Quite where William Butler would have planted his nine rows of beans, or sited his hive of honey-bees, I am not quite sure, as the island appeared to be entirely covered in trees. But I have at least put a place to the words. Only one question remains: is it pronounced Innisfree, or Innishfree?

I also stopped at the Irish Museum of Country Life. Unlike its English equivalent, which is buried in suburban Reading, this is set in glorious countryside near the town of Castlebar in County Mayo. No expense has been spared in bringing to life the harsh realities of rural

*The Lake Isle of Innisfree*

existence (and it can't have been much more than that) in Ireland as it used to be, and to some extent still is. One of the sections was on peat-cutting, showing the remarkable tool that the peat-cutters use to gouge the peat from the bogs. It is part knife, part spade and part scoop, and it is as much in use today as it ever was. On every moor I've driven through, the peat-diggers have been at work, piling up the sods for next winter's fuel.

Deeply traditional and characteristic as it is, I'm still slightly surprised that the climate-change-PC brigade – which is every bit as strong here in Ireland as it is in the UK – aren't trying to get peat cutting banned, given the huge amounts of CO2 that must be released (a) in digging it and (b) in burning it.

Tomorrow is the Irish referendum on the Lisbon Treaty. My money's on a No vote – as a protest against fuel prices. That, in a nutshell, is why referendums are no way to run a country.

## JUNE 13
In St. Patrick's footsteps

On Thursday, I climbed one of Ireland's most famous mountains: Croagh Patrick, near Westport in County Mayo, known familiarly as

"The Reek". On its summit, Ireland's patron saint spent 40 days fasting, praying and throwing the country's entire population of snakes to their deaths, back in the year 441. It is a proper mountain, with a peak shaped like a rocket's nose-cone, but at only 2,500 feet, I wasn't expecting it to be too much of a challenge.

How wrong can you be? It turned out to be by far the most exhausting climb I've ever made – far more difficult than Mount Brandon, Ireland's second highest mountain, down in

*The Reek – an exhausting climb*

Dingle. The way up consists of a broad, deeply rutted, boulder-strewn avenue of scree, which becomes almost vertical on the final ascent to the summit. It was hard to say which was the more painful: the going up or the coming down. I've got two dodgy knees, and by the time I reached the bottom – with, Oh, such a heartfelt sigh of relief – I didn't know which leg to limp on.

Yet this is a mountain climbed by hundreds of people every day, and by over 20,000 in a single day when Mass is celebrated on the summit, on the last Sunday in July. It must be the cause of more voluntarily embraced suffering than any other place in the British Isles. And for why? Because most of those who climb it aren't merely tourists, they are pilgrims. This is a holy mountain, which attracts devout Catholics not just from all over Ireland, but from all over the world. I met one lady who was doing it barefoot, in honour of the Saint. She had painted the soles of her feet with tar, but even so, it must have been excruciating.

There is an Oratory on the summit. I reached it just as the clouds rolled in, blotting out what I'm sure would have been a spectacular view of Clew Bay and the mountains beyond. I'm afraid I didn't walk around the chapel three times, saying my Hail Marys. My grandfather, a fiercely anti-Papist Baptist Minister, would never have forgiven me. But I did take myself off to a respectful distance before opening the can of Inch's cider that I'd thoughtfully brought with me to celebrate the moment.

*... with its due reward*

Then it was off through the mountains and lakes of Connemara to the Renvyle Peninsula. The landscape was strongly reminiscent of Scotland, but it somehow lacks the majesty – the grandeur – of the lochs and bens. The west of Ireland is rough, ragged, hairy-arsed country – a bit like the people who inhabit it. The village of Tully, where I stayed last night, has the most beautiful setting that could be imagined. It also has two of the most downright unpleasant "pubs" it has ever been my misfortune to visit. Both were populated by drunken, swearing locals. I don't much like the F word in any circumstances, but it sounds particularly nasty and brutish, when delivered frequently and indiscriminately in a thick Irish accent.

That said, if there is one campsite that I would recommend to any reader planning a camping holiday in the West of Ireland, it is Renvyle Camping. The site leads directly onto a beautiful beach and offers the most wonderful panorama of mountains, from Slievemore, on Achill, through the Nephin Begg range in Mayo, past my old friend The Reek, to the Twelve Bens of Connemara, which were so forbidding that even St. Patrick gave them his blessing and passed on his way.

Now I have reached Doolin in County Clare, with the remarkable limestone pavement of The Burren behind me and the Cliffs of Moher in front. Clare is undoubtedly the place to be, with my wife Claire due to arrive from Shannon airport any minute. "Keep Clare Clean", demanded a billboard as I crossed the county boundary. I shall do my best!

In the meantime, and reverting to the religious theme, I will leave you with a house in Doolin, which I guess must be owned by an ex-Catholic, who has seen the non-conformist light. It is called "Dunroman"!

PS – see previous comments on likely outcome and significance of referendums

## JUNE 16

On the edge.

The Firbolg were an ancient Celtic race – possibly related to the Belgae – who colonised Ireland sometime around 1000 BC. According to one version of events (and ancient Irish history always owes as much to legend as to record), they were driven from the main island by invading Picts from Scotland, and made their last stand on the Aran Islands, in Galway Bay. There they left behind them a series of "Duns" – circular or semi-circular forts consisting of massive limestone ramparts – the most famous of which is Dun Aengus on the largest of the Aran islands, Inishmore.

Claire and I visited it on a gloriously sunny day on Saturday, and it is indeed a remarkable feat of primitive construction. But also, it struck

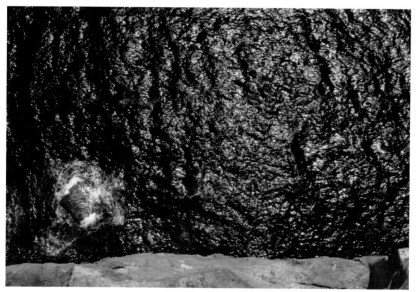

*Over the edge at Dun Aengus*

me, a pretty pointless one. The site of the fort commands no harbour, or river crossing, or settlement. It has been built on the very edge of a 300 foot cliff. There is no water supply and the ground is solid rock. It is the sort of place you might build for your last stand, because, once invested by a besieging enemy, there would be no way out except that sheer drop into the Atlantic. No-one knows if that was indeed the eventual fate of the Firbolg, but they do seem to have disappeared rather abruptly – over the edge of history?

I am glad to say that despite the tens of thousands of people who visit the site each year, there is no safety fence on the fort's seaward edge. The thing to do is to lie flat on your tummy and wriggle yourself up to the edge, so that you can hang your head over the edge of the limestone platform, and look down into the churning waters 300 feet below. It is a stomach-fluttering experience.

Much as Dun Aengus was the last bastion of the Firbolg, so the Aran Islands have long been regarded as the last bastion of true 'Irishness'. The writer J.M. Synge (of "Playboy of the Western World" fame) spent many months there, attempting to learn Gaelic, around the turn of the 20th century, and has left a delightful account of his experiences, which I am reading.

It is, in truth, a wild and barren spot. The landscape of all three islands mostly consists of great sheets of limestone: a geologist's delight, a farmer's despair. On the highest point of Inishmore, next to the light-house, an old cottage has been furnished as it would have been in the old days, complete with earth floor, a peat roof and a bed of filthy rags. It looked all too horribly genuine.

Today, we've been to the Cliffs of Moher, where the Burren limestone pavement sheers off, as it meets the Atlantic. This is another place to be avoided by the vertiginous. Around the visitor centre (which has been dug into the hillside, like an enormous Hobbit's house), there is a paved walkway, protected from the cliff edge by a barrier of limestone slabs. But after about 300 metres, that comes to an end, and from then on westwards, the way is along a narrow, rutted path, which must be hellishly slippery when it's wet, with nothing between you and the Atlantic, 600 feet below. There is a sign, which rather plaintively implores visitors 'please do not go past this point', but it must be one of the most ignored signs in Ireland, and that's saying something.

The cliffs are truly awe-inspiring. Even at 11 o'clock of a Monday morning, there were thousands of people there, most of them from America, by the sound of it, although there were also lots of Germans, French and even Russians. What is it about Ireland that attracts inter-national tourists in such numbers, one wonders? After all, our beauty spots are just as spectacular (think the Scillies, St. Michael's Mount, the Valley of the Rocks, Cheddar Gorge etc), and the weather's better. So why don't the Americans come? At least some of them must have had ancestors from the South-West, and especially from Cornwall.

Our food and drink is better as well. Continuing my search for a decent drop of beer, I'd tracked down a bar in Lahinch that was supposed to offer beers from the Biddy Early brewery. After a fruitless search, we discovered that it had changed its name, and when I asked the waitress if they had any local beers, she said no, "only the usuals". How any country can claim to have a local food culture when the drinks it offers are either mass-produced (Guinness, Murphy's, Smithwick's etc), ersatz (Magners, Bulmers) or imported (the wine, most of it from Chile) is beyond me.

The truth of the matter is that, despite all of the hype, Ireland doesn't have a local food culture. It has an international food culture, promul-gated by celebrity chefs and tourism marketeers, which has been grafted on to the local cuisine, without changing in any way the underlying Irish taste for chips, stodge and fizzy beer. You should only come here for the food if you've got a very fat wallet, and even then don't expect much that is genuinely local.

Having said all of that, Claire and I did eat very well, and reasonably, at the Riverside restaurant here in Doolin, last night. So it's not all bad.

*The three of us at Nagle's Doolin Campsite*

## JUNE 18

*Mannix depression*

Weather systems are well-named. 'Highs' and 'Lows' describe precisely the emotions inspired by their respective arrivals, whilst 'deep depression' speaks for itself. The one that enveloped Carmen and me at Mannix Point, at the bottom end of the Iveragh peninsula, had a peculiarly Celtic intensity, both in its nature, and its effect.

It left me particularly downcast, because it meant that no boats were sailing, and so denied me my one chance, on this trip, of visiting one of the most spectacular of all Celtic sites, the Skelligs: twin pinnacles of rock which jut out of the Atlantic, 12 miles or so out to sea from Waterville. I have a photograph of them on my bedroom wall at home, taken with a long lens when Claire and I visited Kerry in 2004. On the larger of the two – Skellig Michael – one of the most remarkable monasteries

*Storm brewing*

in the world was somehow constructed in the 7th century. It was abandoned some 500 years later but is still, apparently, substantially complete. Perhaps next time.

The weather was so filthy that I didn't venture out of the van until tea-time. Valentia island (another stalwart of 'weather reports from coastal stations') was completely obscured by rain and low cloud, even though it's just across the bay. I resisted the temptation (just) of drinking myself into a state of Celtic oblivion, and busied myself with the computer.

Anyway, when the downpour finally eased, I did my laundry (8 euros, would you believe!) and then headed off into town to buy a newspaper and something for my supper. By great good fortune, I spotted a fish shop, where the owner was filleting some small plaice – "fresh off the boat sorr". I bought some and fried them in butter for my supper and they were quite the best thing I've eaten in the entire journey.

Spirits revived, I headed off on the bike to the little ferry that crosses from Rennard's Point to Valentia. By this time, it was a simply glorious evening, the rain having washed the air clean, and the fuchsia hedges which are such a feature of the west of Ireland fairly blazed with colour as I pedalled along.

The campsite and its owner – who rejoices in the name of Mortimer Moriarty – have won numerous awards, and despite the extortionate cost of using a washing machine and tumble drier, one can see why. The situation is perfect – on the edge of Valentia Sound, looking directly across to the island – and the facilities manage to be both homespun (like a peat fire in the communal reading room) and comprehensive. Assuming that I do return for another crack at Skellig Michael, this is where I shall stay.

Tomorrow, it's the long drive to Dublin, for a ferry to Holyhead early on Friday.

What a wonderful place Ireland would be, if it wasn't for the weather!

*Mannix Point, with the mountains of Kerry beyond*

## WALES - JUNE 21

Land of my great-grandfathers.

I am two miles south-west of Aberdaron, at T Newydd on the very tip of the beautiful Lleyn peninsula. If it wasn't for the driving rain and thick fog, I would be able to see Bardsey Island out of Carmen's back window. The famously nationalistic and unremittingly gloomy Welsh poet, R.S Thomas, was parish priest here for 20 years. Almost everyone speaks Welsh. I am, in fact, so deep into Wales that I've almost come out the other side.

My son George likes to refer to this expedition, a touch sarcastically, as my "voyage of self-discovery", and in one respect at least, that is exactly what it has proved to be. I wrote not long ago that "there isn't a single drop of farming blood coursing through my veins". It appears that I was wrong. Yesterday, after catching the early ferry from Dublin to Holyhead, I stopped off at Llandudno, to visit the only relations on my mother's side of the family – the Welsh side – with whom we have any contact: my second cousin Mary Machin, and her husband Stephen. Mary's mother Lyn was the daughter of my grandfather Daniel's eldest brother, William, and before she died she made a start on piecing together a family tree.

From this, I discovered that the great-grandfather that Mary and I have in common – William Thomas – came from Ty'n y Clwt Farm, near Bethesda. Yes, farm! I don't know any more than that about him, but on the face of it, he would appear either to have been a farmer, or at the very least to have been a farmer's son. So far from there being not a single drop of farming blood in my veins, there could be as much as a whole pint! I shall view myself in a completely different light in future. A. Gibson – descended from a long line of fiercely Welsh farmers. It probably explains a lot!

On Wednesday afternoon, I caught the bus from the campsite at Camac Valley into Dublin. I'm not a great fan of cities, but it has to be admitted that this is a handsome one. I followed the established tourist

*The tart with the cart!*

trail, through Temple Bar, and up O'Connell Street past the Spike to the Post Office, which featured so prominently in the Easter Rising of 1916. I even tracked down the bronze sculpture of Molly Malone in Grafton Street – "The Tart with the Cart", as it is known, and with good reason. She's showing more bosom than you could shake a stick at!

I was just wandering back toward the bus stop, reflecting sadly on the deep irony that a city so famous for its pubs should be so lacking in decent beer, when I spotted "The Porterhouse Brewery", in Parliament Street. I ventured in, and you'll never guess what I spied on the bar? Yes, a handpump, dispensing 100% genuine real Irish bitter, called Sticklebracht, and brewed on the premises. It was excellent, and it is a lovely pub as well. If you're ever in Dublin, don't miss it.

The 200 mile drive from Cahersiveen to Dublin had been surprisingly uneventful, given the inherent dangers associated with Irish major roads, and their crazy run-off areas or whatever it is they're called. You never know what you're going to encounter in them – a brace of female power walkers perhaps (power-walking is big in Ireland), or maybe a pony and trap, a gaggle of cyclists, or even a family having a picnic. Yet none of this stops the heavy lorries from pulling onto these hard shoulders at high speed to allow following traffic to overtake. Whenever you cross a county boundary on a main road in Ireland, you're confronted with a large sign warning of how many motorists have been killed on the roads there in the last year. I'm not in the least bit surprised. At one point, the lorry in front had to veer out of the hard shoulder to avoid a tractor and muck-spreader parked on it just over the brow of a hill. It could have been very nasty.

I'm also intrigued by the way the Irish write their warning signs on the road itself. If you read from the top down (which I guess most of us in England do), the wording appears as:

*Bardsey Island through the storm*

TAKING
OVER
NO
When I first saw it, I thought it was something to do with the Referendum campaign.

I also liked the one on the jetty at Doolin, where the ferries leave for Arran:
OF
PIER
END

Mind you, one of the most striking examples of Irishness I have encountered was here in Wales last evening. There isn't even the ghost of a mobile signal here on the campsite. The only spot for miles around where there is some reception is about a mile down the road – right alongside the BT telephone box!

## JUNE 24
### Talyllyn Ho!

On Sunday, after a storm-tossed night, I made a cautious way through the shrieking gale from Aberdaron to Tywyn. Quite why I picked Tywyn, which is a rather wind-blown, sand-blasted seaside town with nothing in particular to recommend it (a bit like Seaton, but without the charm), for an overnight stop, I cannot now remember. The choice of "Hendy", out of the dozen or so certificated locations in the Caravan Club directory, was a matter of pure chance. I did wonder vaguely whether "Mrs. A Lloyd Jones" might possibly be connected with John Lloyd Jones, whom I have known and respected for many years as one of the most intelligent and forward-thinking leaders of Welsh farming, but given that there must be thousands of Lloyd Jones in the Principality, I swiftly discounted it.

*Carmen at Hendy*

But it was *that* Lloyd Jones, sure enough. I arrived shortly after Sunday lunchtime and was immediately sat down and invited to share a bottle of good red wine with my hosts. We talked of mutual NFU friends, exchanged gossip and discovered a shared frustration with what is happening to the various schemes that have been developed to enable farmers to produce countryside as well as food. John has been Chairman for many years of CCW, the Welsh conservation agency which produced Tyr Gofal, hailed by the former Agriculture Commissioner, Franz Fischler, as "the most successful agri-environment scheme in the Europe". Tyr Gofal has been taken over and ruined by the Welsh Assembly Government, in much the same way as the equally successful ESA scheme is being butchered by Defra to make way for its half-baked "Environmental Stewardship" in England.

In both cases, 20 years of painstaking progress, involving millions of pounds of taxpayers' money, is likely to be chucked away because the conservation bureaucrats who presently call the tune in Defra cannot see beyond the end of their noses. You need pragmatism to find the right balance between food production and conservation. Natural England doesn't appear to know the meaning of the word.

As with many another Welsh farm, tourism is very much the mainstay of Hendy's income. It involves some handsome self-catering cottages and farmhouse b and b as well as the campsite, and appeared to be very much Ann Lloyd Jones' creation and responsibility; a business which she combines with being a sturdily independent member of Gwynedd county council.

Ann apart, Hendy's greatest asset is the Talylln railway, which runs so close to the farm that it even has its own halt. It has the distinction of being the first line in Britain to be taken over and run by volunteers; it was the inspiration for W.S.Awdry's Thomas the Tank Engine; and its appeal is universal.

*The Talyllyn Railway*

I shared a carriage on the Monday morning with an American family (who were also staying at Hendy) who had travelled all the way from Chicago for the thrill of a trip on the Talyllyn. The little trains chug and clank their way up the valley through some of the most magnificent scenery you'll see anywhere (the Dolgoch Falls are a particular delight) and you can go up and down the line all day, getting off and on wherever you fancy, and all for just £12.

*The Dolgoth Gorge above Tywyn*

In the afternoon, I drove to Borth, another undistinguished seaside town, strung out along Cardigan Bay a few miles north of Aberystwyth and, like Tywyn, beset on either side by mobile homes. Borth has one saving grace, and that is its golf course: an old-fashioned out and back links which I have hugely enjoyed playing ever since I first visited, some 16 years ago. I found a decent campsite nearby and by this stage it had become the most beautiful sunny afternoon. I didn't play very well, but the setting more than made up for that. As I hooked and three-putted my way back along the shore, the whole of Cardigan Bay was laid out before me, from the Lleyn in the North, to Cardigan Island in the south.

The only thing missing was some decent surf. That has been the one big disappointment of the trip so far. When I was in Scotland and for most of the time in Ireland, the wind was from the east. Then, when it did switch to the South West, it was so violent, it blew out any swell. I'm now at Whitesands Bay, a mile of so from St. David's, and I've got high surfing hopes for tomorrow.

## JUNE 27

Once in royal St. David's city.

Of all the places I have visited in my travels so far, nowhere has been more charming, interesting and characteristically Celtic than St. David's and the countryside and coastline which surrounds it. The centre-piece of Britain's smallest city (it's no bigger really than a medium-sized village) is, of course, its small but perfectly formed cathedral, which was unusually, but entirely sensibly, built, not on top of what would inevitably have been a gale-swept hill, but at the bottom of a little valley. This means that, approaching the city from the surrounding country-side, all you can see of the cathedral is the pinnacles on top of its central tower. Only when you reach the valley itself is the full glory of the beautifully proportioned cathedral church revealed. Next to it are the romantic ruins of the Bishop's Castle, which the Prince of Wales visited earlier this week, to open the newly restored cloisters. He must have been in his element!

*A Celtic jewel – St. David's Cathedral*

There is something delightfully Celtic about the cathedral. It's not just that it's almost hidden away out of sight in its secret valley, but it was also built on a significant slope (upwards from west to east), the pillars in the nave seem to be leaning outwards and massive stone buttressing has had to be put in place to stop the north side collapsing. No Anglo-Saxon could ever have built a church like this!

Despite (or perhaps because of) its remoteness, St. David's seems to have been something of a hub for Celtic Christianity. St. David was born here, of course. His mother, St. Non, gave birth to him on a hillside to the south of the city, in the middle of a violent thunderstorm. A holy well and a ruined chapel mark the spot.

She then went on to Cornwall to found the church of Altarnun on the edge of Bodmin Moor, which is otherwise distinguished by being the home of the Western Morning News' estimable farming editor, Peter 'Bingo' Hall, before heading off for more missionary work in Brittany.

*St. Non's Well – created when a bolt of lightning struck the ground while she was giving birth to St. David. Must have been an electrifying experience!*

On the other side of the city, close to the handsome beach of White-sands Bay, a stone plaque indicates the site of what was once a chapel dedicated to St. Patrick, to mark the spot where the Welshman who was to become the patron saint of Ireland, set off from his native land. If you are looking for evidence of the links that joined the Celtic cultures in the centuries before the Conquest, there is no shortage of it in and around St. David's.

I've got to know St. David's reasonably well over the last few years, in my role as a director of Farms for City Children. Treginnis Isaf, on the very tip of the peninsula, looking across to Ramsey Island, is the second of the three farms that Clare and Michael Morpurgo set up to take residential visits from inner city primary school-children. I visited on Thursday morning and was delighted to learn from Mike Plant, the farm school manager, that the enterprise is going from strength to strength. A party of 40 or so ten year olds from Dartford in Kent were in residence and had just finished the morning mucking out of goats and pigs. A happier, more polite, genuinely interested and talkative bunch of school kids you never met in all your life.

All this, and a golf course too. The City of St. David's GC celebrated its centenary five years ago and I doubt if it has changed much in all that time. It was ferociously windy, but the views over Whitesands to St.David's head on one side of the bay and Ramsey island on the other, were stunning.

Still no surfing. The sea was far too wild, even for the professionals, let alone for ageing wallowers like me. I was planning to head off to the Gower to try my luck there, but the forecast spoke of unrelenting rain, so I decided to cut my losses and take a few days off at home. Next stop is Cornwall, somewhere near Tintagel, on July 6.

*Carn Llidi and Whitesands Bay from St. David's Head*

# CORNWALL - JULY 6
## Well I'm badgered!

I am at Tintagel and it is pouring with rain, as indeed it has been for virtually the entire week-end. We drove down on Friday morning to Wembury (Claire under her own steam), for the wedding of Diane Lethbridge, who made Taste of the West what it is, and David Hunt, who farms at North Huish near Avonwick. It was the second time around for both of them, but no less happy an occasion for that.

The reception was held at the Langford Court Hotel, a mile or so up the hill from St. Werburgh's. Half of the South Hams farming community seemed to be there. I was expecting the conversation to be angry and about badgers, the BBC having leaked the news that morning that the gutless Minister of a spineless Government has, after dithering for months, finally decided to announce the decision that I know for a fact he made months ago: that there will be no official cull. But the mood was resigned, if not relaxed, and the consensus seemed to be that the best thing to do would be to say as little as possible, let the controversy subside and then just quietly get on with the business of dealing with the source of the infection – within the law, of course!

The hunting fraternity have shown how much can be achieved by stretching the law to its absolute limit without actually breaking it. I can understand the need for a ritual protest, and maybe even for some legal action, but I have never had much confidence in the likely effectiveness of an official cull, given the constraints to which it would inevitably be subject. Vaccination will no doubt provide a solution eventually. In the meantime, if a few thousand diseased badgers are humanely put out of their misery, most country people will be only too delighted.

On Saturday morning, when I went to introduce myself to my hosts at Wembury Cottage Certificated Location, I found them repairing some damage to the door of their garden shed. It turned out that a combination of bolt and padlock had proved no match for a badger determined to smash his way in to get at the bird food stored inside. Cuddly these animals are not. I took particular care to secure Carmen's side door that night, lest word had got around the badger community that I was in the area!

Thereafter, it rained, and rained, and rained. We drove into Plymouth to meet up with an old friend of mine, Tony Oxley, in his favourite mid-morning haunt of the Dolphin on the Barbican. This was the pub made

*Dozmary Pool*

famous by Beryl Cook. Even at 11 in the morning, it is no place for the faint-hearted. Claire was all for ordering a cup of coffee. It would have made a wonderful subject for a Bateman cartoon! After that, more rain and a puncture. Fortunately, there were three decent pubs within walking distance of the campsite.

It was still raining this morning when Claire returned to Langport and I set off for Cornwall. But by the time I'd reached Bodmin Moor (having decided upon an Arthurian theme for the day), the downpour had given way to periodic heavy showers. I stopped at Jamaica Inn and cycled across the moor to Dozmary Pool, into which Sir Bedevere eventually brought himself to cast Excalibur. It struck me as an unexceptional stretch of water, and even though the lowering skies gave the scene a somewhat ominous flavour, I found it hard to visualise the brand being grasped by that arm:

*Clothed in white samite, mystic, wonderful* (as Tennyson has it).

Not that Tennyson placed the scene in question anywhere near Bodmin Moor. His preference was Loe Pool, near Porthleven, not least because it fits in well with Lyonesse being the site of Arthur's last battle.

For myself, I prefer the claims of Slaughter Bridge, near Camelford, where there is now a modest Arthurian centre. I drove past it on my way to Tintagel, having previously paused at the pretty village of Altarnun. With its handsome church (founded, you'll recall, by St. Non, the mother of St. David, who gives his name to neighbouring David-stow) and a head of John Wesley, by the renowned Cornish sculptor, Neville Northey Burnard, it is one of Cornwall's hidden gems.

*A hidden gem – St. Non's Church at Altarnun*

Such is the fame of Tintagel, that it surprised me when I got here that it is just a village. After raining all afternoon, the weather lifted for just long enough for me to visit the castle. It was officially closed, but still mostly accessible, thus saving me the £4.70 entrance fee. The village may be full of tat (although it's a lot better than it was) and its Arthurian pretensions distinctly thin, but it does undoubtedly have a touch of magic about it, which the legendary editor of the Western Morning News, R.A.J. Walling, describes much better than I ever could, in his excellent book "The West Country":

*"The realism of history has no part in the emotion inspired by Tintagel. If these walls were built sheer on the edge of the cliff by some prosaic Norman baron, what of it? The heroism of the British king, his high emprise, the fervour of the lost cause nobly fought, the idealism of an immortal story are the things we recall looking out upon the great ocean and up and down the serried cliff-bound coast with its rich coat of vandyke and emerald and sapphire; and if we come here on a night*

*of moonlight every seabird whose wings or whose cry we hear will be for us the spirit of Arthur which, embodied in a Cornish chough, haunts the scene of his mortal glory waiting for the moment when he shall in a new avatar lead the British race to victory over their Saxon enemies."*

There speaks the true voice of the Celt!

*"King Arthur's Castle", Tintagel*

## JULY 8

Celtic connections

St. Piran, the patron saint of tin miners, if not of Cornwall itself, was an Irishman: a follower of St. Patrick, the patron saint of Ireland. He, of course, was a Welshman. The father of the Celtic church in Scotland was St. Columba, from Donegal. Did these differences mean much at the time? I suspect not. They were all just Celts, speaking more or less the same language, united in opposition to the Norsemen and Saxons advancing ever further from North and East. Many of the Breton saints have strong links with both Cornwall and Ireland, although the flow

*Trevose Head*

does seem to have been predominantly north to south. On the spur of the moment, I can think of no originally Cornish saint who made any sort of mark elsewhere, although that may simply be because the Irish and the Bretons were very much more assiduous in preserving their historical records than the Cornish.

Anyway, in common with virtually all the myriad of Cornish "saints", Piran was essentially a missionary, who set up his 'llan' – a religious settlement – alongside a little stream a mile or so inland from what is now Penhale Bay. In around 550, he built an Oratory, which was over-whelmed by the shifting sands maybe a thousand years ago. By a curious coincidence, it was redis-covered at around the same time – the turn of the 19th century – that the church that was built to replace it was similarly having to be abandoned.

*St. Piran's Oratory, re-buried in the sands*

This being Cornwall, with its fine disregard for antiquity and beauty, the Oratory had no sooner been disinterred than it was ransacked. Eventually, in the early years of the 20th century, they encased it in concrete, giving it the appearance of a particularly ugly roadside garage. So ugly, in fact, that – this being Cornwall – they decided thirty years later it would be better off buried again!

Despite all of that, St. Piran's Oratory remains a place of pilgrimage, not to be missed by any self-respecting Celtic Odysseus. So yesterday, I cycled the six miles from St. Agnes Beacon to Perranporth, and slogged the last three miles along the beach and up through the mighty towans, to pay my respects. It was a grey, windy, gloomy afternoon, which would have been a disappointment in mid-November, let alone in early July, and my left knee was killing me. But I was glad I made the effort. It is an atmospheric spot. In Ireland, it would be crawling with tourists. In Cornwall, I had it all to myself.

I made another pilgrimage this morning – to Knill's Monument, overlooking St. Ives, where we scattered my father's ashes in 1997. I don't know what the old boy would have made of his eldest son touring Cornwall in what he would no doubt have described dismissively as "a

*Knill's Monument, St. Ives*

motorised caravan"; although come to think of it, I do – it would have been "Tcha!" But St. Ives was just about his favourite place in all the world, and all of his four children – myself, Chippy, Adam and Felicity – were taught the rituals to be followed when visiting Knill's Monument. I may have got this wrong – in which case, father, forgive me – but I think the drill is to walk three times around the pediment of the granite steeple, pausing after each circuit to intone: "Old John Knill pray work my will" and make a wish. Or then again, it could be that you have to walk around it three times and then call upon the old boy to grant a single wish. I opted for the former, but kept the wishes modest, just in case I'd got it wrong!

I am installed now not far from Knill's steeple, at Trevalgan Holiday Park, about two miles west of St. Ives. Looking north from the earthwork (modern, I fear) in front of Carmen's bonnet, I can see the top of Godrevy lighthouse and even make out (with binoculars) the campsite where I stayed last night on St. Agnes Beacon, 15 miles north up the stupendous North Cornwall coast.

And you'll never guess what happened this afternoon.... The sun came out! So I tucked my plancha di agua under my arm, packed my wetsuit and swimming trunks into my rucksack, and set off across the fields to Porthmeor Beach and my first surf of the entire trip. It wasn't exactly historic. The waves were as messy and unsatisfactory as a Gordon Brown compromise (and that's the polite simile!), but it was unquestionably a surf.

As I write, we are being engulfed by yet another storm from the West. I am comforted by John Knill's splendid motto, which appears on his monument:

NIL DESPERANDUM!

## JULY 10
Wet, wet, wet

It goes without saying that it rained all day yesterday, although 'rain' seems a singularly inadequate word to describe what we endured. This wasn't soft summer rain; it was cold, hard, slanting winter rain, driven in on a chill westerly gale.

Fortunately, a bus runs every hour from the Trevalgan Farm campsite (which I strongly recommend) into St. Ives, so I decided to console myself with a good lunch, at the Blue Fish, behind the Sloop. I ordered calamari, followed by sea bass with noodles, samphire and chilli jam, off the fixed price £14.95 menu, washed down with a bottle of house Sauvignon. The calamari were exemplary; the sea bass was rather overwhelmed by its accompaniments. The waitress' black thong added considerable further enchantment to the view.

It was still tipping down when I left at 3.00, so I decided to while away an hour or so with a pint and The Times crossword at the Golden

*The Sloop from the Blue Fish – too wet even for the seagulls*

Lion (a Good Beer Guide entry whose doors I had never previously darkened). The all-day drinkers were going strong in the back bar. The focus of conversation was a gentleman who suffers from a speech impediment I had not previously encountered. He was incapable of saying anything just once; it had to be repeated at least three times.

"What was it Pericles did? What was it Pericles did? What was it Pericles did?"

We never did discover.

The conversation became progressively more surreal, as the subject of spinach somehow intruded into a debate on Che Guevara.

"Can Che Guevara save the world? Can Che Guevara save the world? Can Che Guevara save the world? With spinach. With spinach. With spinach."

To which his equally pie-eyed friend replied, with commendable logic under the circumstances:

"Not any more he can't. He's dead. The CIA done 'im in. And bugger your spinach!"

I decided against a £4.75 visit to the Tate St. Ives. Having been left distinctly cold by the contents of the Guggenheim in Bilbao, I didn't hold out much hope of getting my money's worth of cultural inspiration at what is a distinctly poor relation.

It stopped raining at 6.00 precisely. I squelched my way down to the coastal footpath and sat on a bench, to watch the sun move across the waters, and listen to the larks and the sea.

*Sunshine at last, near Zennor*

Today, the weather has been much better. So much so that I fell fast asleep in the afternoon sunshine on Gwynver beach, just down the cliff from what is another excellent campsite (Trevedra Farm near Sennen), and was two hours late for my round of golf at Cape Cornwall. I got round by 9.30.

*Cape Cornwall*

It isn't the greatest golf course in the world (some of the holes are deeply silly), but it does have glorious views. Having played at mainland Britain's most northerly course, just a few miles from one of its two Capes, I felt I was completing the circle by playing at its most westerly, just a few hundred yards from the other Cape. And I bettered my handicap by a shot.

Tomorrow, the Scillies.

## JULY 12

### On Wingletang Down

I rather think that the Isles of Scilly is my favourite place in all the world. I love my home in Somerset, of course; the Blackdown Hills has a very

*The slightly sinister "Nag's Head" on Wingletang Down, St. Agnes*

special place in my heart; Braunton Burrows is magical; Dartmoor moves me as nowhere else; and I have a great fondness for the blue sea and golden beaches of the south west corner of Portugal. But I guess that if you were to invite me to choose a place in which to spend a final holiday before the great umpire in the sky draws stumps, the Isles of Scilly it would have to be.

For islands so beautiful, it is quite remarkable how unspoilt they have remained. The air is pure and clean, the sea is clearer than a mountain stream, the sky on a clear night is a wonder to behold. And within every island, there are the most remarkable contrasts between the sub-tropical calm of the lagoon-facing coasts, and the wildness of the cliffs and heaths battered by the open sea.

I would visit all of the inhabited islands in the course of my final holiday (and Samson as well), for they are all beautiful in their different ways: cosmopolitan St. Mary's; the slightly rough diamond that is Bryher; the white sands and crystal waters of St. Martins; even time-share Tresco has its charms, quite apart from the Abbey Gardens. But the island on which I would base myself would be St. Agnes. It is the smallest of the main islands, the most southerly, the most Celtic and, to my mind, the most characteristically Scillonian.

You can walk its coastline in a morning, as I did yesterday. Starting at the smart new quay, with its formal gardens, I walked anti-clockwise, to the cricket ground, on which I would so love to play, and on to Periglis, with its perfect crescent of white sand, little church, lifeboat station and whitewashed cottages. Troytown Farm is next, with its campsite, its farm shop and the new house for the coming generation of Hicks' (almost everyone who lives on St. Agnes is a Hicks), as featured on "An Island Parish" on the BBC during the winter.

Then it is out onto Wingletang Down, with its fantastical rock formations, springy turf, ancient sites and the ever-restless sea. I paused at the 400 year old Troytown Maze and threw a coin into St. Warna's well, into which – according to what I'm sure is as baseless a story as it is scurrilous – the locals used to throw pins and pray for shipwrecks. There is a little beach in the south west corner of Wingletang called Porth Askin.

*Porth Askin*

The last time we were there, Claire found herself pursued by an amorous seal (well, it was an easy mistake for him to make!). This time, I swam on my own, and there were no seals. The water was cold, but not breathtakingly so.

I made a point of visiting Horse Point, which I'm pretty sure is the most southerly point in the British Isles, before turning north past Beady Pool, to the sandbar which joins St. Agnes to Gugh (off which most of the sand has been washed by last winter's storms) and finally, the Turk's Head, which is Claire's favourite pub, and where I ate a whole Scilly crab, so fresh that it was still warm from the boiler. The sun was out by now, and I dozed the after-noon away on Gugh. It was a day made in heaven.

From the Turk's Head, looking past St. Agnes' new quay towards Tresco

After all of that, my visit to Land's End this morn-ing was a bit of a come-down. It is by no means the most spectacular headland in Cornwall and any sense of being at the end of the world has been entirely destroyed, not just by the hotel, but by the spectacularly tacky "shop-ping village" and sundry other "amusements", which have been allowed to grow up alongside. The contrast with the smart and sophisticated visitor centre at the Cliffs of Moher, or the way in which the French have sought to protect the wildness of the Pointe du Raz by keeping the tourist facilities at a discreet distance, is by no means to Cornwall's advantage.

Just reverting to the Scillies for a moment, it is a mistake to think of them as offering Cornishness in its purest, most distilled form, in the way that the Aran Islands do with Irishness. They do have a strongly Celtic core, of course, but it has been seasoned and enriched over the centuries by the myriad of people who have washed up on Scilly's shores – often quite literally – and have chosen to remain. They do say that one of the reasons why the islands are so different from each other is the influence of shipwreck. The inhabitants of St. Agnes tend to be short and dark, on account, so the theory goes, of the Spanish ship that was wrecked there in the sixteenth century. The people of St. Martins, by contrast, are tall and blue-eyed, by courtesy of the men who made it to shore when a Norwegian ship went down, many moons ago.

While I was waiting at Lands End airport to board the little aeroplane that would carry me to Scilly, a Cornish lady came up to me and said "you must be a Scillonian". I had to confess that I wasn't. But given that Scillonians have a well-deserved reputation for being handsome, unfailingly courteous and well-spoken, I took it as a considerable compliment.

A final word about the campsite – Trevedra Farm. It is the best of the 25 I've stayed at so far, bar none. The fields are level, the views are superb ( I can actually see the Scillies in the distance out of Carmen's windows as I write), the farm shop sells all sorts of local goodies, including excellent pasties, the showers and loos are clean and smart and there is a lovely sandy surfing beach just half a mile away down the cliff.

It's also only a couple of miles from the little town which really does offer the essence of Cornwall, and that is St. Just. It has two really good pubs (the Star and the King's Head), one of the best pasty shops in the Duchy (Warrens) and an excellent fish and chip restaurant, which is where I'm headed on my bicycle to buy my supper. I might just have a pint as well, while I'm there!

*St. Martin's*

## JULY 15

*Choughed!*

I was walking back from Kynance Cove to Lizard village on Sunday evening when my attention was caught by a group of particularly noisy black birds in a grassy clearing in the Cornish heath. "You jackdaws have got a lot to say for yourself", I said to them. Except that, no sooner were the words out of my mouth, than I realised they weren't jackdaws at all. Jackdaws don't have red beaks, or red legs. These birds – praise all the saints of Cornwall – could only be choughs.

Fortunately, I had my little digital camera with me and took a handful of rushed shots. At this they flew off, alighting again about 100 yards away, so I followed them, and took a couple more photographs, before the five of them took wing and headed off towards the cliff top. Given that

*The spirit of King Arthur? A chough on the wing*

this is one of the rarest birds in Britain – extinct here from the early 1970s until their reintroduction in 2001 – I still couldn't quite believe my luck. As soon as I got back to Carmen, I transferred the pictures from camera to computer, to study them more closely. There was no mistake: the downward curving red beaks, the glossy black plumage, the red legs. These were choughs: the emblem of Cornwall; the bird in which the soul of King Arthur himself is supposed to reside.

They probably chat to each other in a strong Spanish accent (Asturian, I suspect!), as that is the country from which they were reintroduced. But as far as I am concerned, these were the genuine, legendary, Cornish article. If I'd seen a Phoenix on the wing, I couldn't have been more surprised or pleased.

That was the highlight of a glorious Sunday, in which I clocked two new breweries (Penzance and Lizard), swam at Gwynver in the morning and Kynance Cove in the afternoon, and basked in the well-nigh unbroken sunshine. The sea at Kynance was crowded with children, most of them wearing wet-suits. It struck me that we are in danger of breeding a

*Kynance Cove on a glorious summer's day*

generation of wimps, who won't go into the sea without a wetsuit because "it's too cold". Besides which they're denying themselves one of the supreme sensory pleasures, of cool water on warm skin. I've got nothing against wet-suits for surfing, but swimming in them is (one must assume) like making love using an old sock as a condom.

"Henry's Campsite", in Lizard village, is very different from the wide open spaces of Trevedra, but just as delightful. It feels almost as if I'm camping in a garden; a garden in the Isles of Scilly, at that. We are surrounded by palms, echiums, agapanthus and big white daisies. Chickens poke around between the tents. The pitches are marked out by massive granite gateposts. And, best of all, the little campsite/farm shop sells Spingo, from the Blue Anchor in Helston, which has the oldest working brewery in Britain.

It was gloomy and overcast on Monday morning as I walked first to the Lizard Point, and then onto the Most Southerly point itself, complete with the Most Southerly cafe, Most Southerly gift shop, Most Southerly car park and Most Southerly public toilets. This isn't a place which hides its location under a bushel. The sea was flat calm, and when the fog rolled in, each blast from the lighthouse station's foghorn reverberated mournfully for fully ten seconds off rocks and cliffs and glassy ocean.

*Most southerly!*

I lunched on a pasty from "Ann's Famous Pasty Shop" and I have to say that Warrens of St. Just has a serious rival. The pastry is a sort of cross between short and puff – just as with the incomparable (in my humble opinion) Ivor Dewdney's pasties in Plymouth (the Exeter ones are a deeply inferior imitation).

This afternoon, I cycled to Coverack, via Cadgwith and Kennack Sands. The sun emerged briefly from behind the scudding mist, but then disappeared again. Goonhilly Downs, across which I cycled, is as bleak a heath as you could meet, but in the little valleys that run down to the sea, I saw something almost as rare as a Cornish chough – half grown elm trees. Presumably, being cut off by the heathland, they're far enough away from other elms to escape the wretched beetle. But it was a bitter-sweet moment, because it struck me that my three children are both too young to have seen a fully-grown English elm in all its glory in the past, but not young enough to have any realistic hope of seeing one in the future.

*Blogging away, with refreshment to hand!*

So that is the end of what I think I can safely call the British Isles leg of the trip. I plan to leave for Brittany in late August, and in the meantime, when I get home, will offer some halfway stage reflections.

## JULY 17

Reflections at the halfway stage

I have driven 3,500 miles, stayed at 28 campsites, played 284 holes of golf, chalked up 17 new breweries and visited goodness knows how many new pubs. Yet, despite the fact that my route has taken me down virtually the entire western seaboard of the British Isles, and included scores of beautiful beaches, I have been swimming only seven times, and surfed (feebly) but thrice. From that you will gather that, whilst the weather has been fine, it has only occasionally been what you might call "beach weather" and not once baking hot.

Which, of course, is precisely what one should expect on the Celtic coast. If I'd wanted unbroken sunshine, and a warm sea that laps rather pathetically at one's feet, then I would have gone to the Mediterranean. If there's been a disappointment, it's not been the weather conditions, so much as the sea conditions. In Scotland and Ireland, the wind was mostly from the East. There was no Atlantic swell to speak of. Wales provided one spectacular storm, but then there was no subsequent offshore breeze to smooth the churning waters into slick-backed, lace-crested rollers. The Cornish waves offered the most promise, but conditions never really progressed beyond what the serious surfers call "messy".

So, have I enjoyed it? For the most part, undoubtedly. I have to confess that there were one or two days, when the rain beat down remorselessly, and the forecast offered little prospect of an improvement, and I was being bitten to death by midges, that I wished myself back at my cottage in Langport. But the weather was only seriously bad for a handful of days, and never for more than a day at a time. To be able to see the Scottish Highlands in bright sunshine was a particular joy.

What it has been is an experience. Even at this halfway stage, I have been to so many beautiful places, travelled through so much magnificently wild and wonderful countryside, explored the physical remains of so much real or imagined history, as to leave me with memories to last a lifetime.

What have I learnt? That Carmen is longer than she appears, especially when you're reversing into a parking space! That I really can't putt! That camper-vanners wave to each other when passing on the roads. That Irish roads are the worst in Europe. That, for all the gloss of re-invented cuisines, the food of the western seaboard of the British Isles is mostly pretty dire. And that the Celtic communities of western Britain really do have a lot in common. One thinks immediately of their spirituality; a fondness for religion and the supernatural; a tendency to excess, of drink especially; an inexhaustible sense of humour; and something of a chip on their shoulder when it comes to the English! To what extent these shared characteristics are the result of a shared racial background, or a shared harsh and elemental physical environment is a matter for debate. My money would be on the latter.

In these terms, the Irish are the most "Celtic" and the Scots the least. Cornwall's genuinely Celtic characteristics – as distinct from heritage – are now largely confined to the far West. The Welsh are almost a race apart: the senior Celtic nation, particularly in the context of Celtic Christianity. It was from Wales that the missionaries travelled – led by St.

Patrick – to convert the heathen Irish. And it was then the Irish, having embraced the new religion with a quite astonishing fervour, who invaded the West of Cornwall, bringing their missionaries with them, many of whom subsequently moved on to Brittany. That seems to have been the rough sequence of events and it does give credence to the theory that the last stand of the old "British" people against the Saxons – which produced the legends of Arthur – took place in Wales, rather than Cornwall.

Anyway, that's quite enough idle theorising and cod history to be going on with. I have, as I said, hugely enjoyed the trip so far, and am looking forward enormously to the start of the next stage, in Brittany at the end of August.

The best day? Well, that would have to be the Isles of Scilly.

The never before visited place to which I would most like to return? That would be a toss up between remote Durness and the silver sands of Camusdarach. The Isle of Arran was beautiful as well, as indeed were the Aran Islands.

The best golf? Unquestionably, Machrihanish, a truly glorious golf course, although for value for money, you probably couldn't beat the 15 euros it cost to play at Achill.

The best pub? The Porterhouse Brewery in Dublin, which brewed its own good beer, and stood out from the ocean of keg porter and bitter that surrounds it like a good deed in a naughty world.

The worst day? Aberdaron in the storm was pretty bad, and so was St. Ives in the downpour. But undoubtedly the greatest disappointment was the foul weather that stopped the boats going to the Skelligs on the one day when I could have made the trip.

And Carmen? She was as Rosinante to Don Quixote – faithful, dependable, a constant companion. She'll now be taking a well-earned rest, before we set off for Plymouth and the Roscoff ferry on August 24.

# BRITTANY - AUGUST 27
On the road again

I write at Camping Les Abers, looking out through Carmen's windscreen to the clitter-clatter of low, rocky, somehow desolate islands that fringe the North-West coast of Brittany. In the distance, a faint pink glow enlivens the otherwise unremitting grey of sky and sea, offering

*Celtic to the core – a holy well in the Parish of Lamber near St. Renan*

hope of a brighter day tomorrow.

The campsite is at Aber-Wrach (as in Aberystwyth), just west of Landeda (as in Lanivet).The district of Leon (from Caerleon), where I am presently based, was originally divided up into Dumnonee (as in Devon) and Cornouaille (as in it goes without saying). Even the Breton language, now so jealously guarded, was largely imported from Cornwall and Wales, from the fifth century onwards.

But when we talk about 'Little Britain', which is what Brittany literally means, we need to remember that the 'British' in question were strictly of the ancient, Celtic variety. The Irish, Welsh and Cornish who colonised Brittany in the Dark Ages were looking for somewhere to escape from the Saxons and Vikings, pressing ever westwards. Armorica, as it was then known, was a bleak, infertile, windswept, storm-ravaged, thinly populated peninsula largely cut off from the rest of civilised Europe. It made the Cornish, the Welsh and the Irish feel entirely at home!

Anyway, by reaching Aber-wrach by way of Wales, Cornwall and a sea crossing to Roscoff, I have been travelling in ancient, not to say sacred footsteps. St. Pol-de-Leon, just a few miles from the ferry terminal, is named for the same Paul who gave his name to Paul, near Penzance, and whose chapel here at Aber-wrach I visited earlier today. He was a Welshman, of course!

Unlike Paul, who no doubt made the crossing on a millstone or a cabbage leaf, I travelled in some style, on the Brittany Ferries flagship, the Port Aven. It is a trip I have made many times, and I was looking forward to its rituals, not least the steak-frites in the self-service restaurant as the boat clears the Eddystone lighthouse (and not a moment before!). The food on Brittany Ferries is not exactly world-class, but it is at least French, which is a good start.

I looked up at the board above the servery, just to check that it was on. Sure enough, there it was: "Entrecote grille". But what was that in the small print underneath?

*"Origin S. America"*

I looked again, just to check it hadn't read "S.Armorica", which is what one might have expected on a boat run by the fanatic gastro-patriots who are the Bretons.

But no, S. America it undoubtedly was, and S. American it undoubtedly tasted – stringy and gristly. I have rarely been more disappointed with a meal in my entire life. My thoughts turned to Alexis Gourvennec, the Breton farmer who founded Brittany Ferries and who sadly died earlier this year. He was arguably the most effective militant farmer who ever lived. He bullied the Government into funding the Roscoff ferry terminal and he dragooned the notoriously cussed small farmers of Brittany into joining his co-operative – the SICA, as it then was – on pain of having their crops burnt.

The likes of Handley and Haddock are but pigmies to Gourvennec's colossus. He transformed farming in Brittany. The magnificent crops of cauliflower, onions, leeks, potatoes, lettuce, shallots, broccoli and artichokes –

*Alexis Gourvennec – a pocket battleship of a farming leader*

especially artichokes, although he never did manage to persuade Plymothians to love them! – that I drove past on my way here this morning are a tribute to his passion, skill and belligerence.

I don't know about him spinning in his grave. I'm surprised that he hasn't burst forth from it: to blockade the ferry company which has so betrayed his legacy and to threaten to burn its boats, one by one, until every last kilo of foreign beef has been tipped into the grey Atlantic.

That apart, the journey across was relatively uneventful. I stayed last night at Mogueriec, not far from Roscoff, on a campsite which, apart from me and Carmen, was eerily deserted. Even the owner made his excuses and left. It was a disturbed, as well as a lonely night. I was just dropping off to sleep when my ears were assailed by the unmistakeable whine of a mosquito, on its final approach towards my neck. Now, if there is one thing in life that I detest even more than split infinitives and the mispronunciation of west country place names it is mosquitos! I had the light on a flash, armed myself with a rolled up Times, and went in search of the little beggars. I got two in the first sweep, two more later on, and one final buzzing menace was nailed to the window frame just before dawn. Conducive to sleep this was not, so I have invested in an electronic device which promises "45 nuits" of mosquito-free bliss. We shall see.

One thing that that Bretons have not, fortunately, inherited from their Celtic cousins further north, is their cuisine, which is Frankish to the core, albeit using the magnificent local ingredients. I cycled to Prat-ar-

*A perfect Breton supper*

Coum this afternoon to buy some oysters for my supper. A dozen of the freshest, plumpest, most sea-flavoured bivalves as could be imagined set me back just 4 euros 50. On Sunday, at Lyme Regis, the Hix Oyster and Fish Bar had much less fresh oysters on offer at £1.75 each!

I was given a leaflet describing the local attractions when I arrived this afternoon. From this, I learned that, near Plougerneau, there is a "Seaweed Museum". Now that's got to be up there, alongside Barometer World (near Okehampton, if you're desperate), as one of the most unlikely tourist attractions in Western Europe!

## AUGUST 29
Lights to my path

Ushant! A name to strike fear into any mariner's heart: an island of violent storms, savage reefs, treacherous tides, impenetrable fogs and tearing Atlantic gales; rising low but menacingly, like a crocodile in a whirlpool, on the edge of the continental shelf where the Bay of Biscay joins the English Channel; at the very western tip of France. "Ouessant", they call it here. "The Westernmost" is how I like to translate it. Mind you, the Celts called it Enez-Eussa – the Isle of Terror – and the channel that separates Ushant from Molene is From-Veur – the strait of fear!

Except that, today, when I made the long anticipated sea crossing from Le Conquet, there wasn't so much as an Atlantic zephyr, let alone an Atlantic gale, either to stir the waters into their customary anger or, more to the point, to shift the low, misty cloud that has enveloped the north-west coast of Brittany like a grey shroud these last four days.

But I made the best of it – hiring a bike which enabled me to see most of what is, without the assistance of the more violent among the elements, a rather flat and dull island. Ushant's hallmark is its light-houses. There are five of them in all: three at the outer edges of the reefs that stretch out towards one of the busiest sea-lanes in Europe, and two on the island itself. I paused for a glass of cider and a packet of crisps on the Pointe de Pern – the most Westerly point in France – where two ruinous pylons and a crumbling stone barn provided, respectively, electricity and a gigantic steam-powered fog-horn for the Phare de Nividic, just offshore. With its ceaselessly churning sea and gigantic masses of granite, the peninsula reminded me powerfully of Wingle-tang Down on St. Agnes.

*At the most westerly point in France – the Pointe de Pern on Ushant. In the background, the now derelict equipment for powering the lighthouse*

But even more impressive is the Phare du Creac'h, reputedly the most powerful lighthouse in Europe, if not the world. It is black and white and massive. Du Creac'h is to normal lighthouses what the Millennium Eye is to fairground wheels. This is the daddy of them all!

And thereby hangs a theory of mine. The Bretons are big on lighthouses. There are hundreds of them. On the Ile de Vierge – Virgin Island – they've built not just one, but two of them, one the tallest in Europe. Now if that's not making a Gallic, or better still a Celtic point, I don't know what is! Because this fondness for tall straight things, penetrating the very skies above, goes back a long way in these parts. Around every corner is a standing stone, sometimes made decent with a cross on the top, but by no means always.

Yesterday I stopped off at the tallest menhir still standing in Brittany, at Kerloas near St. Renan. It has two protuberances, about a metre from its base, against which newly married couples were once wont to rub their naked bodies: on one, the man, so as to beget a son; on the other, the woman, so as to be the boss of her household. One of them still looks suspiciously shiny and worn, and I'll bet I can guess which!

*The menhir of Kerloas – with that suspiciously shiny bump!*

Be it sacred or profane, lighthouses seem to me to have much the same significance in modern Brittany as menhirs did in the old days. What finally convinced me of that was when, after returning from Ushant, I cycled down to the Pointe de St. Mathieu, at the western end of the Rade de Brest. There I found the still substantial ruins of a Benedictine Abbey – with an enormous lighthouse standing right alongside the entrance to the nave!

I am camping at Les Blancs Sablons, overlooking the estuary (Aber or Rade) which has given Le Conquet its sheltered harbour. It's a long way round to the town by road, but no distance at all on foot or bicycle, across the long, low passarelle, which I've discovered is French for footbridge. The beach here is superb. Even under murky cloud, swimming yesterday afternoon was a delight, and there's surf as well. Le Conquet is a pretty, unspoilt little fishing port. There may be pleasanter corners of North West Brittany, but if there are I've yet to discover them.

*Le Phare de St. Mathieu – presumably Cardinal Newman was asked to advise on its siting ("lead kindly light......")!!*

And if you detect a slightly more upbeat tone as these notes reach their conclusion, there's a very good reason. The sun has a last broken through. I celebrated by roasting myself an enormous veal chop (and drinking a toast to Compassion in World Farming as I ate it), which was quite one of the best things I've eaten all year.

A final postscript to Wednesday's dispatch: St. Paul of Aurelian did not arrive in Brittany at Roscoff, as I suggested. He came ashore on Ushant. I visited the spot today. He was also indirectly responsible for the original chapel at Pointe de St. Mathieu. In fact, one way or another, I seem to be treading in his footsteps much as I did in those of St. Columba in Scotland and Ireland. I wonder if St. Paul built lighthouses as well?!

## AUGUST 31

A Laver of a crab

I am at Camaret, on the Crozon peninsula, which juts out from the Brittany coast south of Brest rather like a giant anchor, albeit one with

*Classic Crozon: looking north from the Pointe de Penhir to the Pointe de Toulinguet – and the beach where you're not supposed to swim!*

all sorts of odd-shaped prongs at its business end. Crozon appears to be off the main Anglo-German tourist routes. I saw as many English cars en route to the Cap de la Chevre this morning as I would expect to encounter French cars on the way to the Lizard. My appalling linguistic skills are therefore more of a handicap than ever. I can work out in my own mind what I want to say. It is when my interlocutor asks me a question in reply that I go all to pieces. Pathetic, isn't it?

Yesterday, the shone sun, for the first and – if the weather forecast is to be relied upon – possibly the only day of this leg of the trip. I spent the first part of the afternoon basking, swimming and reading on the almost deserted beach below the campsite. Then, when the incoming tide left nothing more than rocks to perch upon, I took myself off to Camaret-sur-Mer on the bike.

It is a pretty little fishing town, with a long line of shops, bars and restaurants along the harbour. Not so much chic as neat and tidy. Having chosen a restaurant at which I would sup later, I went to explore the standing stones at Lagatjar, which rather suffer in their impact from the modern housing estate which has been built alongside, and then onto Pointe de Penhir, one of several dramatic headlands that stretch out in all directions from Camaret and Crozon. It was still sunny and warm, so I decided on a final swim before supper, on what looked like an inviting beach. But when I got there, I was confronted by huge notices saying "Baignade Interdit" by order of the Council. However, no-one seemed to be taking the slightest notice of them, so I didn't either.

My meal at La Voilerie was OK, but no better than that. The fish soup was exemplary but there was something slightly odd about the crab mayonnaise. There appeared to be the correct number of arms, legs and other bits and pieces, but the pincers in particular were of strikingly different dimensions. I concluded that either my crab had been an assemblage from more than one crab, or, like Rod Laver, it had spent a lot of time playing tennis, leaving one forearm much larger than the other!

*A suburban Carnac – the stone rows at Lagatjar*

At any event, whilst, at 10 euros, it might have been cheaper than my crab at the Turk's Head on St. Agnes, it was certainly no better.

With half a bottle of a modest Muscadet, the bill came to 26 euros, which represented reasonable value. It's the booze that's become so expensive here in recent years. A 250 ml 'pression' – that's less than half a pint of fizzy lager – will now set you back 2 euros 40, even in a scruffy tabac, and a glass of wine is the same price. That's the equivalent of something like £4.20 a pint at the current exchange rate, and it's frightful stuff as well. Wine in the supermarkets and 'caves' is still marginally cheaper than in England, but I've yet to find better value over here than the magnums of Chilean cabernet that Tescos were selling for £5 a throw just before I left. I even brought a couple with me; now that's coals to Newcastle if you like.

The weather hasn't held. By the time I was making my way back from Camaret the thunderclouds were building, and the most tremendous storm broke over the peninsula at 2.00 this morning. I've never heard anything quite like it. It sounded as if God was hurling wardrobes around in the attic, and the lightning was so incessant that the country-side appeared floodlit. And my God, didn't it rain!

*An ominous sky – the night before the great thunderstorm over Camaret*

Today has been mostly grey and drizzly, although the sun did break through just after lunch. I cycled via Crozon and Morgat to Cap de la Chevre, which is about 12 miles south of here. If there is such a thing as a 'typical Breton small town' then Crozon is it: narrow streets of ancient houses leading off from its central 'Place' where a market was in full swing right outside the church. It has to be said that the fish and vegeta-bles here are in a completely different class to anything on our side of the channel. One of several fish stalls had the most beautiful turbot on sale for 26 euros a kilo. I was sorely tempted to buy one for my supper, but then it dawned on me that it wouldn't be improved by several hours in a rucksack on my sweaty back.

The Cap de la Chevre is my third cape of the trip so far. It translates as 'Cape Goat', which doesn't have quite the same ring to it as Cape Wrath or Cape Cornwall. Nor am I entirely sure which are the two seas whose meeting point it is supposed to mark. Presumably the Bay of Biscay and the English Channel, although Point de St. Mathieu (which I can see out of Carmen's windscreen as I write on the other side of the Rade de Brest) would be a much more obvious choice. But it is a magnificent headland and does command spectacular views on every side, from the Pointe du Raz and the Ile de Sein in the south to Ushant in the north. My distinguished predecessor (in the sense of being a Celtic traveller) R.A.J.Walling was so impressed with the cape that he declared it "the true finis terre – the end of the earth" (The Magic of Brittany – highly recommended).

Now it is raining again and it is time for supper. After moules for lunch at Morgat, I've bought myself some steak – local, of course, but with English mustard!

## SEPTEMBER 2

*A la recherche de temps perdu*

I am a terrible one for nostalgia. I love nothing better than to wallow in lost but happy times, or what Henry Williamson called 'ancient sunlight'. So if my exploits of the last couple of days seem to have something of a sentimental journey about them, you will understand why and, I trust, be appropriately forgiving.

I stayed last night at Audierne, about five miles from the Pointe du Raz. It is a pleasant fishing village cum holiday resort, tucked just in behind the coastline, around a little estuary. The last time I was here was on the second part of my second honeymoon. As the storm clouds gathered yesterday evening, I cycled into town from the campsite at Kersiny Plage to revisit old haunts and bring happy, sunlit memories back to life. The town didn't seem to have changed one bit, and, sure enough, there, out by the break-water, was the Bras-

*The Hotel du Roi Gradlon at Audierne*

serie de Grand Large, where I had downed my first pression as a newly re-married man, on a gloriously sunny evening back in May 2001. My reverie was rather rudely curtailed when I discovered it was shut!

However, the Hotel du Roi Gradlon (the Breton equivalent of King Arthur), where Claire and I had stayed, overlooking Audierne's long white beach, was very much open, so I had a drink there instead. It is a rather unprepossessing building, but in a glorious situation. A double room with a balcony and fabulous views out to sea will set you back 79 euros, which strikes me as about as decent value for money as you will find in these parts, especially as the food is excellent as well. I can recommend both Audierne and the Roi Gradlon unreservedly – and that's nothing to do with rose-tinted spectacles!

Today, I drove through relentless and torrential rain to Trevignon, which is a few miles south west of the handsome fishing port of Concarneau. This is another place which holds the happiest of memories. I used to come here with my three children, Joanna, Becky and George, when we holidayed in Brittany back in the 1990s. There is a whale-shaped rock about a hundred yards offshore to which we used to swim out and then dive off – George, aged about six, included! The poor little lad almost

*Now you know what you've got to do!*

drowned getting there, but once he'd made it, he would hurl himself time and again into the deep blue water, as if it was the greatest thing in the world.

I was determined to do it again, for old times' sake, but although the sun had come out by this stage, the overnight storm had left a tempestuous sea in its wake, and whilst I managed to swim out to the rock, I couldn't clamber onto it. But it was still good to be back on what is one of my favourite beaches in all the world. It is a perfect crescent, with granite rocks on either side, and the quartz in the white sand makes it sparkle with a million tiny points of light when the sun shines, as it did eventually this afternoon. Happy days!

However, you will be reassured to learn that I have not entirely been neglecting my Celtic duties in all this self-indulgence. Yesterday, en route from Camaret to Audierene, I visited three of the most famous places on the Brittany tourist trail. First stop was at the Menez Hom, which isn't quite the highest point in Brittany, but probably is the closest thing they've got to a sacred mountain, like Croagh Patrick. At just over 1,000 feet, it is a modest eminence and, the French being the lazy beggars they are, they've built a road almost to the top. Still, the views back over the Crozon Peninsula and out across the Bay of Douarnenez are stunning, and the weather was clear enough to be able to appreciate them.

Then it was onto Locronan, which is the Breton equivalent of Castle Combe, or Milton Abbas or Clovelly: a model village, all cobbled streets and old stone houses with hanging baskets and window boxes, grouped around a handsome church. Locronan has featured in dozens of films and television programmes including, most implausibly, Roman Polanski's 'Tess of the D'Urbervilles'. It doesn't look remotely like Dorchester, but it's charming enough.

My final stop was at the Pointe du Raz, supposedly the most westerly point in mainland France, and the Breton equivalent of Land's End. It is visited by millions of people every year and although the inevitable shopping village is less tacky and much less further away from the cliffs than at Land's End, it's not really the place to go to commune with nature at its wildest and most Celtic. Having said that, the views out to sea, across the truly frightening tidal race that gives the headland its name, to the island of Sein in the distance, are well worth the trek and the 6 euros you have to pay to park. I took a picnic, which included a cheese and tomato baguette into which I bit rather too energetically,

*At the Pointe du Raz, looking past La Vielle toward the Ile de Sein in the distance*

squirting tomato all down my shirt and shorts.

This was a pity, because I was enjoying myself, having actually found a sheltered and reasonably secluded spot, over-looking the Baie de Trepasses (so called for the number of drowned corpses that used to wash up there). Beneath the waves here lies Brittany's Lyonesse: the lost city of Ys, which was drowned when King Gradlon's wicked daughter opened all the sluice-gates. The Arthur/Gradlon legends are by no means identical, but they do have many common features, including Merlin. They are, of course, two trees from but a single root, and a root, what is more, that was essentially historical, rather than mythical.

## SEPTEMBER 4

### The road to Hell – or Heaven?!

I was going to conclude the Brittany leg of my journey with a visit to the extraordinary 'alignments' at Carnac, and a crossing on the ferry from Quiberon to Belle Ile en Mer. But Carnac is strictly speaking pre-Celtic and Belle-Ile – whilst undoubtedly living up to its name – I have visited before. The clincher was the weather forecast, which is dire.

So I decided to cut short my visit by a day and catch a ferry to Belle-Ile's little sister, the Ile de Groix, where I'd never yet set foot. The only drawback was that the ferries sail from the deeply unlovely city of Lorient. It was built in the seventeenth century as a jumping off point for the French East India trade – hence the name – and, from what I can gather, its architecture has always been more functional than decorative.

Lorient does, however, have a most magnificent, well-protected, natural harbour, and it was the obvious choice when Hitler was

*Lorient's premier tourist attraction – the indestructible U boat base!*

deciding where to base his Atlantic U-boat fleet. In the final stages of the war, the city was bombed unmercifully by the Allies. They flattened everything – except the U-boat base, which was built of concrete several metres thick. It is now a rather sinister tourist attraction: "the strongest fortress of the 20th century" is the boast, and I wouldn't doubt it for a moment. It is also quite spectacularly ugly and menacing, and is thus entirely in keeping with its surroundings.

However, there was no avoiding Lorient if I wanted to get to the Ile de Groix, so I sought out the nearest campsite to the city, so that I could cycle to the ferry terminal, rather than having to find an over-sized parking space for Carmen. In this respect I was lucky. I lighted upon Armor Plage, which although now just a suburb of Lorient, does have several good beaches (from one of which I swam in yesterday's windy sunshine) and an excellent municipal campsite. I cannot image any English campsite-owner choosing the name Camping Seaweed, which is how Camping des Algues translates, but I've not been too oppressed with kelp, and in every other respect it is ideal: just behind the beach, on the edge of what is a pleasant little town, and reassuringly protected by German gun emplacements!

The weather was blustery and grey, as I set off shortly after dawn to catch the only ferry of the morning. They say that French traffic systems are much friendlier to cyclists than English ones. Not in Lorient, they aren't! My route consisted almost entirely of dual carriageways, along the edge of which I was obliged to creep, hoping to God that any mad Frenchman turning right would spot me in time. I'd got to within a mile or so of the Gare Maritime, when I suddenly spotted a road sign consisting of a big red circle with a bicycle symbol inside it. There was no indication of any alternative route, and by this stage it was raining hard. It took me at least another half an hour to reach my destination, with no help whatsoever from signs, road markings or my fellow road users, and by that time I was soaked.

However, all was well in the end. I warmed to the Ile de Groix as soon as I discovered that its patron saint is none other than our own St. Tudy, who travelled with St. Brioc from Wales, founded his church near Wadebridge and then went on to the Ile de Groix. This connection was sufficiently heart-warming even to take the sting out of the Ile de Groix's chief military claim to fame, which is that the women of the island, led by their priest and in the absence of their menfolk, who were all out fishing, succeeded in frightening off a heavily armed English fleet in 1703 by dressing up as men and using milk churns to simulate cannon. What brave lads those English must have been!

I hired a bike and completed a circuit of the entire island, pausing at

Locmaria for moules frites and a demi of vin blanc for lunch. I visited the two lighthouses at either end of the island, Pen Men and the Pointe des Chats, I looked hard into Port Saint Nicholas, without making a sound, to see if I could spot "The Quiet Fairy" to whom this is home, and I looked deep into the Trou de l'Enfer, surprised that there should be two Hell Holes (Lorient being the other) in such close proximity. When I reached the sheltered south-west of the island, I even went for a swim off Les Grands Sables, which has the rare distinction for a beach of being convex, rather than concave.

*Les Grands Sables on Groix – lovely, and with a touch of pink, even under grey skies*

There is an old Breton proverb which avers that "Who sees Groix, sees his joy", and for all the grey skies, blustery wind and intermittent downpours, I was pretty joyful. It isn't as smart as Belle-Ile and none of the beaches compares with the magnificent Port Donnant, but it is pretty, has no pretensions, is largely unspoilt and, when the sun is shining, I'll bet it's a little heaven on earth.

This is my last night in Brittany. Tomorrow, I start the long trek south to Asturias, where I hope to arrive on Saturday evening. I don't feel I've in any way done Brittany justice. But then you would probably say much the same even if you spent an entire summer here, let alone just ten days. There is just so much coastline to see, so much culture to soak up, so much wonderful food to enjoy and so many beautiful places to visit – Lorient not included. Every August, they hold the "Inter-Celtic Festival" here. If it was anywhere else, I might be tempted to go.

A culinary note on which to finish: French supermarkets having never apparently heard of either mint sauce or redcurrant jelly, I have taken to accompanying my coteaux d'agneau (of which I am inordinately fond) with a large spoonful of my wife's blackcurrant jam. Like Gibbo and Groix, it is a match made in heaven!

## ASTURIAS - SEPTEMBER 6

It never rains...

Bloody typical! You drive completely unscathed for 600 miles through flood, tempest, mad Polish lorry drivers, umpteen peages and even an inspection by the Spanish border police; then, as you're inching towards your selected pitch among the pine trees – crunch! The hem of Carmen's rather voluminous skirt had become entangled with a low-lying, jutting out railway sleeper, with predictable and doubtless expensive results. I cannot now open the side door, but she is at least still driveable.

Or she would be, if it wasn't for the other little problem that I detected, when I came to get my bike down from the rack at the back. Where the rear number plate should have been was a blank, grey space. The plate had been there when I left my overnight campsite at Castets, a few miles north of Bayonne, no doubt about it. But somewhere in the ensuing 220 miles it had evidently been shaken, or possibly flushed, from its moorings, by the bumpy Spanish roads or the incessant deluge. I retraced the last few miles between here and Comillas, where the road had been particularly bumpy, but to no avail. So I rang NFU Mutual International Rescue (cue Thunderbirds theme music) and got, not Virgil or Lady Penelope but a rather baffled French woman, to whom I explained my predicament. I am still awaiting her call back.

Still, there could be worse places to be marooned. San Vicente de la Barquera, on the coast about 35 miles west of Santander, isn't quite in Asturias, but it is a very handsome town, with two fine bridges and a magnificent sixteenth century ducal palace. I am looking across the estuary at it now, with the houses of the town clustered at its feet and the Picos de Europa behind it in the distance (in truth, that last bit is poetic licence, because although I know that the Picos are indeed somewhere

*View from the campsite – San Vicente de la Barquera, with the Picos in the background*

out there in the distance behind the Palace, I can't actually see them on account of the low cloud and heavy rain!)

However, it has to be said that after my twin misfortunes I wasn't really in the mood to enjoy the series of explosions, accompanied by air-raid sirens, which emanated from the town's lofty fortress. It would appear that some sort of fiesta is taking place. Mr Grumpy wishes them joy, although he won't be amused if the amplified striking of the town clock goes on throughout the night!

Asturias and Galicia are the odd ones out in the co-called "League of Celtic Nations" in that their Celtic languages have not survived. As far

*San Vicente at night – shame you can't hear the music or the gunfire!*

as I can gather (and I stand to be corrected) their claim to be Celtic rests on the North-West coast being the final refuge of the Celtic Iberians, when the Romans finally conquered the peninsula in about 200 BC. Somehow or another they clung to the coastal fringe of

Northern Spain, and there they have remained, cut off from the rest of the country by the Picos and other formidable mountain ranges, with their own very distinctive customs, cultures, cuisines – and climate, which tends to be sunny in the morning and wet in the afternoon.

Legend has it that as the Romans pushed ever further north and west through Spain, some of the native Celts took to the sea, and ended up in Ireland, possibly as the Fir Bolg, or whoever it was who built Dun Aenghus and similar remarkable stone forts, or possibly just as a smattering of settlers, cast ashore on a distant land. I think I tend towards the latter.

Of connections between Celtic Northern Spain and Cornwall, I could find no trace, until my mother (learned lady that she is) recalled some lines from Milton's Lycidas, in which the poet mourns the death of his friend, drowned in the Irish Sea, and wonders where his bones might have been carried:

> *"Whether beyond the stormy Hebrides*
> *Where thou perhaps under the whelming tide*
> *Visit'st the bottom of the monstrous world;*
> *Or whether thou to our moist vows denied*
> *Sleep'st by the fable of Bellerus old,*
> *Where the great vision of the guarded Mount*
> *Looks towards Namancos and Bayona's hold."*

Bellerus is an old word for Cornwall, the Mount is St. Michael's, between which and the Spanish ports of 'Namancos and Bayona's hold', there is nothing but open sea. Even in the sixteenth century, it would seem to have been accepted that the Celtic nations looked to each other, in every sense.

I bought myself a splendid pork chop in San Vicente this evening, and am feeling slightly more mellow, having consumed it with local beans and carrots. But it has still been a pretty rotten day.

## SEPTEMBER 8

On giving it best

With a heavy heart, I have decided to return home early, with the Celtic characteristics of Galicia and Portugal still unexplored. The immediate excuse for thus bottling out is the three day (so far) delay in obtaining a replacement number plate for Carmen, plus the damage to her nearside, which makes it impossible to open the door, and means I have to clamber in and out of the driver's compartment.

However, the truth of the matter is that I am travel-weary after the long slog south and really rather lonely. Being on one's own is not a problem, when you can drop into the nearest pub or golf club and either pass the time of day with whoever may be there, or simply listen to other people's conversations. But when you cannot understand a word they're saying, or vice versa, you do feel a bit out of it, especially if there is no Times or television to help one while away the uneventful hours. So the prospect of driving several hundred miles through remote, inhospitable (so they say) Galicia, in a damaged van, with no company and a distinctly iffy weather forecast was not, I am afraid, one that ultimately appealed.

I knew that the game was up when I woke up this morning, pulled back the curtains to reveal a blameless sky of the brightest blue – and felt my spirits lift not a millimetre. I am sure that Galicia is fascinating, and I deeply want to visit Porto and the Celtic sites of Northern Portugal, but both will have to wait until I can persuade someone to come with me.

In the meantime, the weather has been ironically blissful. Today has been by far the hottest day both of the trip and of my summer. I spent large parts of it in the sea, trying to cool off. This was pleasant enough at the time, but has left me with a blocked left ear. Although even that has its consolations, as it is helping to muffle the deafeningly loud music that is pounding out across the estuary towards the campsite, on account of the continuing Fiesta. Last night, the disco went on until 2.30! The very helpful man in the campsite reception warned me that I might be woken early tomorrow morning. God knows what that may involve. Probably yet another volley of deafening artillery shells, fired from the battlements of the fortress.

The town clock has a most melodious chime, reminiscent of the hours being struck on a spinet or, yes, a melodion. But at what appear to be random hours of the day, this is the signal for the aforementioned howitzers to open up over the bay, frightening the dogs and shattering the reveries.

However, you must not get the impression that I dislike Northern Spain. Very much to the contrary. The scenery is spectacular, the people are kindly, the food is much better than in Brittany and only two thirds the price, and the sea is wonderfully clear and almost silky smooth to swim in, even when there's a decent swell running, which there certainly has these past three days. The surf has been by far the best of the entire trip.

Tomorrow, a taxi is due to arrive at the campsite at 9.00 to take me to an unnamed destination, where a new number plate should await me. Assuming that we don't end up driving to Madrid or San Sebastian, I then intend to catch the bus to Oviedo, the capital city of the Principality of Asturias, to sample what the real Carmen promises me will be a "Pantagruelic" feast of Asturian specialities at El Raitan. (No, I didn't know what it meant, either. Turns out that it's from a 'gigantic prince' called Pantagruel, in Rabelais. But then Carmen always did have a better grasp of the English language than most of us in the NFU for whom it is our native tongue!)

In the meantime, I have been drowning my sorrows with some of that Breton bottle-conditioned beer that I mentioned a few days ago. The Duchesse Anne was excellent – beautifully malty, without being sweet, well-hopped, amber-coloured and quite strong. The Belle Ile was a bit of a disappointment. Despite having left it to settle for the whole morning, it was chock full of sediment when I opened it at lunchtime. It settled down eventually, and turned out to be a rather heavy, malty brown ale – the sort of beer that Newcastle Brown doubtless was before it was debased.

And if you've deduced from that last paragraph that one of the reasons for my early return home is that I'm pining for a decent pint of good old Westcountry beer, you'd be spot on!

## SEPTEMBER 11

Thus far...

I caught the bus from San Vicente into Oviedo yesterday. For a round trip of 200 miles, the fare was 17 euros. And it was well worth it. Oviedo, the capital of the Principality of Asturias, is a handsome, well-proportioned, if slightly claustrophobic city. The streets are all lined with buildings at least ten storeys high. You can barely see the sky, let alone any landmarks. It took a long time for me to find my bearings. Most of the central shopping area has been pedestrianised, and is paved with marble the colour of a Spanish dawn. Walking on it in my M and S loafers produced the most frightful squeaks and squeals!

*Oviedo Cathedral*

Having said all of that, the area around the Cathedral is lovely: ancient, narrow streets, lined with restaurants and sidrerias; leading off into little squares, like the Plaza Trasscorales, with its bronze of La Lechera – the milkmaid – and in which, more to the immediate point, was situated the restaurant where I had set my heart to dine on a veritable feast of Asturian specialities. Only two problems: the restaurant didn't open until 8.00 and the last bus was due to leave at 8.45. So I contented myself with wistfully jotting down the list of things I would have eaten, had circumstances allowed:

Cream of crab soup; Pote – beans, greens, pork and blood pudding; Fabada – the national dish of Asturias – a quite delicious bean and pork stew; braised boar with potato croquettes; rice pudding, crepes and pastries.

All this for 32 euros, in one of the smartest restaurants in the city.

There is one consolation: I am several pounds lighter than I would have been if I'd got the other side of that lot!

I followed the tourist trail, to the cathedral, with its 9th century chapel, and then roused myself to climb the seemingly endless hill which leads to two of the most ancient churches in Spain: Santa Maria del Naranco and San Miguel de Lillo, both also dating back to the 9th century. They were worth the climb: both beautifully proportioned in their different ways, and built in a style which I'm told was unique to Asturias. I bought a ticket for 3 euros which entitled me to go inside both churches – except that it didn't. They both remained firmly locked. It turned out that if I wanted to see inside I would have to wait until a sufficient 'groupo' had assembled to make it worth the guide's while to show us around. He, meanwhile, was having a pee in the hedge, and as the commentary would be in Spanish, it frankly didn't seem worth waiting for.

*The 9th century church of San Miguel de Lillo, on the mountain overlooking Oviedo*

So down the hill I strode, in search of supper. I decided eventually to try one of the many sidrerias in the Calle Gascona. Cider is the Asturias national drink. The locals appear to consume nothing else. Cider-drinking is a ritual conducted with an almost religious solemnity and attention to detail. First is the 'escanciar': in your right hand, you hold the uncorked bottle, stretching your arm as high as it will go. In your left, the broad-brimmed glass-beaker, which you hold as low as you can, slightly tilted, so as to maximise the distance between bottle and glass. Then you pour, and if you're any good at all at it, you pour with the utmost nonchalance, looking up at the sky and whistling a happy tune, confident that years of practice will direct the golden stream unerringly, not merely into the glass, but onto the side of the glass, just below the brim. The idea is that the long drop will maximise oxygenation of the cider, producing a gentle, almost creamy effervescence in the drink.

But that's only the half of it. Only about half an inch is poured at any one go. The recipient is required (and I use the word advisedly) to drink most of it, and then hurl the last few drops against the side of the bar, off which it will drain into a gutter. This is called the "culin" and the logic this time is that, cider drinking being a group activity, by swilling out the glass with cider, you have disinfected it for the next recipient of the escanciar.

It is, as you can imagine, a picturesque business, which involves the waste of a prodigious amount of perfectly good cider. I would hazard a guess that more cider is poured away in Asturias each year than is consumed in any of the other Celtic nations, with the possible exception of Brittany. It was when I first visited Asturias in 1994, that, with my late and much lamented brother, Chippy, we discovered this extraordinary business. We took to it with some enthusiasm! He was much better at the escanciar than I was, but I did my best to make up for it with the violence of my culin!

That was in typical rough and ready rural sidrerias, whose floors were literally awash with cider. In the posher parts of Oviedo, they have to strike a careful balance. So the barman pours (expertly, of course) your cider, and only the standers-at-the-bar are encouraged to chuck the remnants in the gutter. The place still stank of cider, but it was smart enough to charge some pretty fancy prices. I accompanied my bottle with anchovies, peppers and caballes cheese – classic Asturian cuisine. The Olde Cider Bar at Newton Abbot this was not!

And thereby hangs a tale. It was visiting Asturias in 1994 and encountering the fierce pride with which they nurtured and protected their regional specialties, like fabada, that gave me the idea of starting Westcountry Cooking, to encourage chefs and restaurateurs to make a point of using our own wonderful ingredients, in dishes that speak as profoundly of the South West as Asturian cooking does of this beautiful region. I like to think that it had a small influence on everything that has happened since.

Apart from one or two thunderstorms, the weather has been hot and sunny. I have been surfing. Three to four feet and clean, is how I think the professionals would describe it.

On Tuesday morning, I was taken by taxi into Santander to procure Carmen's temporary number plate. The taxi driver, inevitably, was called Manuel. He had no English and I have no Spanish. We proceeded at a truly frightening speed, Manuel making phone calls to various

*The beach at San Vicente in early morning sunshine*

friends and family, the Spanish definition of 'hands-free' appearing to mean no hands on the steering wheel. He struck me as a sociable soul, who clearly wanted to make conversation with his passenger "Gillsaw", as he called me. Football came to the rescue. We exchanged the names of Spanish footballers playing for English clubs, accompanied by facial expressions, shakes of the head or thumbs up to indicate approval or otherwise.

Anyway, we secured the number plate and, although it is the wrong colour, I trust it will serve. It is stuck on with parcel tape, which may or may not survive the storm that is blowing in from the Atlantic as I prepare to drive to Santander to catch the ferry for home, with very mixed feelings.

## SEPTEMBER 15
Journey's End

The Bay of Biscay entirely lived up to its reputation for the journey home. The Pont Aven is a big ship, with everything that modern maritime design can provide in the way of stabilisation. But by mid-evening, she was rolling and juddering in the swell like the Balmoral

*Plymouth Hoe – a sight to gladden the heart of any true Westcountryman*

on a rough crossing from Ilfracombe to Lundy. A clear majority of passengers took refuge in their en suite facilities. The smug brigade, of which I was happy to be part, had the run of the bars and restaurants. There were some very sorry sights the following morning.

I set the alarm for 4.00, reckoning that that would be about the time that we passed Ushant, so that I could see the great lighthouse of An Creac'h in action. It was a good guess. When I got up on deck, the very first thing I saw was the great white beam piercing the night sky, flanked by the red lights of La Jument to the south and Le Stiff (I kid you not!) on the north end of the island. It was a memorable sight. Sadly, the ship was being tossed around too violently to get much of a photograph, but I did my best. I barely slept a wink after that. The beds on the Pont Aven are excruciatingly uncomfortable, even by ferry standards.

We were an hour or so late arriving at Plymouth, but at least the sun was shining. It had been pouring with rain when we'd left Santander, which made me feel happier about the decision to cut short the trip than has been the case subsequently. Jammed door and dodgy number plate notwithstanding, I should have soldiered on through Galicia.

However, what's done is done, and it has still been a fascinating trip. All told, I've driven just over 5,000 miles through Scotland, Ireland,

Wales, Cornwall, Brittany and Asturias, staying at 37 campsites. In an idle moment (and there were plenty of them) at San Vicente, I decided to rank the campsites, according to setting/view, facilities, proximity to beaches/golf courses/good pubs and value for money. The joint winners were Trevedra Farm at Sennen, and Tully Beach Camping and Caravans, on the Renvyle Peninsula in the far west of Ireland, but several others, including Kersigny Plage, Trevignon, Durness, Camusdarach, Gairloch, Tramore Beach and Achill Island were only a point or two behind.

From best campsite, it was but a short step to best days, best meals and best moments.

Among the former, it was a dead heat between my visit to the Isles of Scilly, on a glorious July day, and the day I spent in West Wales, travelling on the Tallylln Railway and golfing at Borth and Ynyslas, also under cloudless skies. Honourable mentions also for St. David's, golf at Machrihanish, my trip to the pub with no beer at Inverie and a swim from the silver sands of Camusdarach, the visits to Ushant and to Inishmore in the Aran Islands, and the first proper day of the entire trip, when I travelled by ferry and minibus to Cape Wrath and played golf in the evening sunshine looking out across the stunningly beautiful sands of Balnakiel Bay.

My best meals were probably those I cooked, or prepared, for myself: the fried plaice at Caheerviseen, the oysters and Muscadet at Les Abers and that magnificent veal chop at Le Conquet. My crab at the Turk's Head on St. Agnes was unquestionably my best meal out.

Best moments? Well, my first sight of "the most beautiful beach in Scotland", Sandwood Bay, after a four mile hike, has got to be up there, as has a four iron across a wave-lashed chasm to the final green at Durness, walking out onto Tramore beach on a sparklingly blue and silver Sunday afternoon and the warmest of Welsh welcomes that I received from Ann and John Lloyd Jones on arriving at Hendy. But I guess the pick of the bunch has to be that moment, near Kynance Cove, when I realised that the noisy birds I'd happened across weren't jackdaws, but were choughs: rare, precious, quintessentially Celtic choughs. If I'd encountered the ghost of King Arthur, I could hardly have been more pleased. (And then again, perhaps that's precisely what I had done?)

And the worst? I suppose that would have to be crunching Carmen against the railway sleeper, precipitating as it did the abandonment of the last stage of the trip. Apart from that, my blackest moment was when I reached my first peage on the A10, just south of Nantes. It was pouring with rain and there were long queues of cars and lorries, all simmering with Gallic impatience. But I'd watched the couple in front carefully, and leant confidently across the cab, to pluck my card from the slot in the machine. Except that when I looked, it wasn't there! The bloody machine had broken down! With half of France waiting and hooting behind me! In a state of flat panic, I climbed out of the cab, to give the machine a good kicking. It was then that – thank God! – I spotted that there was a second dispensing slot, at lorry driver height, and poking out of it was the ticket I so craved. Rarely in my life have I been quite so relieved!

But what, you may well ask, of the avowed purpose of the journey which was, as I recall, "to explore the links between the peoples of Europe's western seaboard"? That there are such links – at least between the "British" Celts – is obvious, in language, religion, culture, climate and geography. But that certainly does not mean that all Celts are the same. The various tribes are as different from one another as they are from other so-called "races", like the Anglo-Saxons, Franks or Vikings. The most obvious example of this is the North and South Waleians. This came home to me most vividly when I was talking to a short, dark, swarthy Pembrokeshire farmer, who prides himself on his Celtic ancestry. "Celtic Odyssey, is it", he said, with a note of disbelief in his voice. "I never realised you were a Celt".

"Oh yes", I replied. "More than 50 per cent. All my mother's family were from Anglesey".

"Ah", he said, the light dawning. "Anglesey. That explains it."

Having said that, it is possible to argue that the generality of Celts do share some characteristics, chief among them probably being a fundamentally passionate nature. They are instinctive, rather than necessarily rational, in how they think and act. They are driven by spirit and soul as much as by logic and analysis. They also all have something of a chip on their shoulders: Irish, Welsh and Scots about the English; Bretons in relation to the French; and Asturians when it comes to the Spanish.

One thing they do all share is the glorious Atlantic seaboard, and its rather less than glorious climate. It would be surprising if this had not produced both a deep sense of man's insignificance in comparison with the immensity of sea, mountains and sky and a certain fatalism in the face of the unrelenting elements. Against that background, it is not to be wondered at that religion, both pagan and Christian, has always played so strong a part in the life of the Celts. If there is one thing more than any other that united the British Celts it was Celtic Christianity.

As for what the trip has taught me about myself – my "voyage of self-discovery", as my son George called it – I think it is probably that, for all my Welsh ancestry, I'm not really Celtic at all! I'm as much of a typical tight-arsed, list-making, home-loving, beer-drinking Englishman, as I am a passionate, instinctive, soulful Celt. And besides, I really cannot stand that awful Irish/Breton folk music – "all that fidde-de-dee stuff", as my wife Claire calls it. Not that I don't have a well-developed emotional side. A Welsh or Cornish male voice choir can move me to tears. But I'd sooner go to the dentist than sit through a concert by the Dubliners.

What I am is a Westcountryman. There is no finer sight in all the world than the tors of Dartmoor as the ferry nears Plymouth. The more I travel, the more I appreciate how deeply fortunate I am to have been born and lived most of my life in the South-West of England.

But it's been what I've experienced, more than what I've learned, which has made the trip so wonderful. The mountains, the cliffs, the seascapes, the moors, the beaches, the crosses, the dolmens – and just the occasional pub or golf-course!